SOCIAL AND BEHAVIORAL SCIENCES

REPORT OF THE
PROJECT 2061 PHASE I
SOCIAL AND BEHAVIORAL
SCIENCES PANEL

by Mortimer H. Appley
and Winifred B. Maher

71628

AMERICAN ASSOCIATION
FOR THE ADVANCEMENT OF SCIENCE

1989

Founded in 1848, the American Association for the Advancement of Science is the world's leading general scientific society, with more than 132,000 individual members and nearly 300 affiliated scientific and engineering societies and academies of science. The AAAS engages in a variety of activities to advance science and human progress. To help meet these goals, the AAAS has a diversified agenda of programs bearing on science and technology policy; the responsibilities and human rights of scientists; intergovernmental relations in science; the public's understanding of science; science education; international cooperation in science and engineering; and opportunities in science and engineering for women, minorities, and people with disabilities. The AAAS also publishes *Science*, a weekly journal for professionals, and *Science Books & Films*, a review magazine for schools and libraries.

ISBN 0-87168-346-6

AAAS Publication 89-05S

Library of Congress Catalog Card Number: 89-101

Printed in the United States of America

CONTENTS

ACKNOWLEDGMENTS

On behalf of the Board of Directors of the American Association for the Advancement of Science, I wish to acknowledge with gratitude the many useful contributions made by the members of the Phase I Social and Behavioral Sciences Panel to the first stage of Project 2061.

The eight panel members were most generous with their time and efforts over a two-year period in developing their response—as presented in this report—to the complex question of what young people should know about the social and behavioral sciences by the time they complete their high school education. The board is also very grateful to Mortimer H. Appley, who chaired the panel and, in collaboration with Winifred B. Maher, wrote the panel's report.

During this essential first stage of Project 2061, the Social and Behavioral Sciences Panel was one of five scientific panels charged by the AAAS with developing independent reports on five basic subject-matter areas. At the same time, the Project 2061 staff in conjunction with the National Council on Science and Technology Education was preparing a separate overview report—*Science for All Americans*—that was able to draw on the conclusions reached by the individual panels.

We also want to extend our thanks to the many people who assisted the panel in the course of its deliberations—the consultants, the national council members and other reviewers, and the Project 2061 staff.

Finally, it is appropriate to note that Project 2061 is indebted to the Carnegie Corporation of New York and the Andrew W. Mellon Foundation for their overall and ongoing support of our various Phase I efforts.

Sheila E. Widnall
Chair, Board of Directors, American Association for the
    Advancement of Science

PHASE I SOCIAL AND BEHAVIORAL SCIENCES PANEL

Mortimer H. Appley   (Panel Chair) Visiting Scholar in Psychology, Harvard University, and President Emeritus, Clark University

Jill K. Conway   Visiting Scholar, Science, Technology, and Society, Massachusetts Institute of Technology, and President Emeritus, Smith College

John T. Dunlop   Professor of Economics and Lamont University Professor Emeritus, Harvard University

Ann F. Friedlaender   Dean of Humanities, Massachusetts Institute of Technology

Jerome Kagan   Professor of Developmental Psychology, Harvard University

R. Duncan Luce   Distinguished Professor of Cognitive Science and Director of the Irvine Research Unit in Mathematical Behavioral Science, University of California, Irvine

Rosemarie Rogers   Professor of International Politics, The Fletcher School of Law and Diplomacy, Tufts University

Nur O. Yalman   Professor of Social Anthropology, Harvard University, and Curator, Middle Eastern Ethnology, The Peabody Museum

Panel Staff: Winifred B. Maher, Lecturer, Harvard University Extension School

FOREWORD

This report is one of five prepared by scientific panels as part of Phase I of Project 2061. Each of the panel reports stands alone as an independent statement of learning goals in a particular domain. In addition, the reports contributed to *Science for All Americans*, a Phase I report that cuts across all of science, mathematics, and technology.

The work of the Social and Behavioral Sciences Panel was to reflect on all aspects of the social and behavioral sciences—their nature, principles, history, and future directions—and to produce a set of recommendations on what knowledge and skills are needed for scientific literacy in these fields. The other panels focused in a similar way on the biological and health sciences, mathematics, the physical and information sciences and engineering, and technology.

In considering this report, it is helpful to see it in the context of Project 2061 and to be aware of the manner in which it was generated.

The American Association for the Advancement of Science initiated Project 2061 in 1985, a year when Comet Halley happened to be in the earth's vicinity. That coincidence prompted the project's name, for it was realized that the children who would live to see the return of the comet in 2061 would soon be starting their school years. The project was motivated by a concern that many share for the inadequate education those young Americans will receive unless there are major reforms in science, mathematics, and technology education.

Scientific literacy—which embraces science, mathematics, and technology—has emerged as a central goal of education. Yet the fact is that general scientific literacy eludes us in the United States. A cascade of recent studies has made it abundantly clear that by national standards and world norms, U.S. education is failing too many students—and hence the nation. The nation has yet to act decisively enough in preparing young people—especially the minority children on whom the nation's future is coming to depend—for a world that continues to change radically in response to the rapid growth of scientific knowledge and technological power.

Believing that America has no more urgent priority than the reform of education in science, mathematics, and technology, the AAAS has committed itself, through Project 2061 and other activities, to helping the nation achieve significant and lasting educational change. Because the work of Project 2061 is expected to last a decade or longer, it has been organized into three phases.

Phase I of the project has established a conceptual base for reform by defining the knowledge, skills, and attitudes all students should acquire as a consequence of their total school experience from kindergarten through high school. That conceptual base consists of recommendations presented in *Science for All Americans* and the five panel reports.

In Phase II of Project 2061, now under way, teams of educators and scientists are transforming these reports into blueprints for action. The main purpose of the second phase of the project is to produce a variety of alternative curriculum models that school districts and states can use as they undertake to reform the teaching of science, mathematics, and technology. Phase II will also specify the characteristics of reforms needed in other areas to make it possible for the new curricula to work: teacher education, testing policies and practices, new materials and modern technologies, the organization of schooling, state and local policies, and research.

In Phase III, the project will collaborate with scientific societies, educational associations and institutions, and other groups involved in the reform of science, mathematics, and technology education, in a nationwide effort to turn the Phase II blueprints into educational practice.

Each of the five panels was composed of 8 to 10 scientists, mathematicians, engineers, physicians, and others known to be accomplished in their fields and disciplines and to be fully conversant with the role of science, mathematics, and technology in the lives of people. The panelists were different from one another in many respects, including their areas of specialization, institutional affiliations, views of science and education, and personal characteristics. What made it possible to capitalize on the rich diversity among the panelists was what they had in common—open minds and a willingness to explore deeply the questions put to them.

The basic question put to the Social and Behavioral Sciences Panel was: What is the social and behavioral sciences component of scientific literacy? Answering this question—difficult enough in itself—was made more difficult by the conditions, or ground rules, set by Project 2061. Abbreviated here, these were:

- *Focus on scientific significance.* Identify only those concepts and skills that are of surpassing scientific importance—those that can serve as a foundation for a lifetime of individual growth.

- *Apply considerations of human significance*. Of the knowledge and skills that meet the criterion of scientific significance, select those that are most likely to prepare students to live interesting and responsible lives. Individual growth and satisfaction need to be considered, as well as the needs of a democratic society in a competitive world.

- *Begin with a clean slate*. Justify all recommendations without regard to the content of today's curricula, textbooks, state and school district requirements, achievement tests, or college entrance examinations.

- *Ignore the limitations of present-day education*. Assume that it will be possible to do whatever it may take—design new curricula and learning materials, prepare teachers, reorganize the schools, set policies, or locate resources—to achieve desired learning outcomes.

- *Identify only a small core of essential knowledge and skills*. Do not call on the schools to cover more and more material, but instead recommend a set of learning goals that will allow them to concentrate on teaching less and on doing it better.

- *Keep in mind the target population—all students.* Propose a common core of learning in technology that can serve as part of the educational foundation of all students, regardless of sex, race, academic talent, or life goals.

Taking these ground rules into account, the members of the Social and Behavioral Sciences Panel met frequently over a period of nearly two years to present and debate ideas and to consider the suggestions of consultants. The panel members prepared working papers and revised them in response to the criticisms of reviewers. This process—which also included meetings with the chairs of other panels—led to the preparation of this report.

The task ahead for the United States is to build a new system of education that will ensure that all of our young people become literate in science, mathematics, and technology. The job will not be achieved easily or quickly, and no report or set of reports can alter that. I believe, however, that this report on literacy in the social and behavioral sciences, along with the other panel reports and *Science for All Americans*, can help clarify the goals of elementary and secondary education and in that way contribute significantly to the reform movement.

F. James Rutherford
Project Director, Project 2061

PREFACE

This is one of five panel reports commissioned under Phase I of Project 2061, an undertaking of the American Association for the Advancement of Science. Project 2061 is intended to identify science and technology training goals appropriate for U.S. high school graduates of the future and to translate those goals into educational specifications.

The purpose of Phase I has been "to build an intellectual base for science education and to produce a compelling statement of what ought to constitute the science, mathematics, and technology 'content' of courses for all children passing through our elementary and secondary schools." The question posed to and by each panel was: "Out of all the possibilities, what science and technology is most worth learning by all young people by the time they leave high school?"

It should be noted that the Phase I panels were asked to identify and recommend content for learning, not to specify a curriculum. The panels were given five criteria for justifying their recommendations: knowledge for its own sake, illumination of human meaning, improved success in individual work and the economy, increased social responsibility, and enhancement of the experience of youth. These criteria reflect the broad goals that underlie universal public education in a free society.

The charge given to the Social and Behavioral Sciences Panel by Project 2061 was to cover fields such as "developmental and social psychology, sociology, economics, statistics, mathematics, political science, public opinion polling, cultural anthropology, archeology, linguistics, speech and language, psychiatry, psychoneurology, cognitive science, history of science, ethics, and science journalism."

Of critical concern to the Social and Behavioral Sciences Panel has been the fact that the treatment of these fields in the school curriculum, unlike that of other science fields, has so far been sparse, or at best uneven. Often, only by the good graces of some biology or physical and health education teachers have students below the college level had any exposure to even limited aspects of the psychological sciences; and almost never are they involved in the scientific study of such subjects as the self in a social context or the comparative study of societies, cultures, and social forms and institutions (perhaps excepting political) and their influence on behavior—although such subjects are often dealt with anecdotally in literary study.

The separate treatment of "social studies," as opposed to social sciences, implies that the scientific approach may not be needed in such areas. As a consequence, the student may fail to understand the importance of the rigorous application of scientific methodology in studying such dynamic processes as the interaction of human needs and the means and consequences of their fulfillment or denial.

Thus, the orderly extension of the scientific approach to the study of social and behavioral events and processes, as envisioned in Project 2061, is in itself an extremely important directive to curricular planners. It makes possible the filling of a critical gap in the use of science as a means of understanding nature—namely, by including human nature and human institutions as proper subjects of scientific study.

To this end, the reader's attention is drawn to Appendix A, which contains a discussion of important aspects of the application of the scientific approach to social and behavioral phenomena. In fact, the reader may wish to explore this topic before beginning the report proper.

Mortimer H. Appley
Chair, Social and Behavioral Sciences Panel

SECTION 1

ORIENTING CONCEPTS

Scientific study of individuals and societies provides insights into the nature of human behavior, thought, and emotion. However, it is seldom clear to students how such study is conducted. One way for them to understand how investigators come to grips with the phenomena they study is to examine the concepts they employ. Accordingly, we start here by describing a dozen general concepts utilized by social and behavioral scientists. Although there is no universal agreement on the definitions and range of applicability of particular concepts, especially when used across areas of study, those described here were chosen to help elucidate how social and behavioral scientists approach their subjects. (Descriptions of additional useful concepts and principles appear elsewhere in this report. It should be noted that many concepts overlap in meaning and, to an extent, represent different ways of describing and understanding the same or similar processes.)

LEVELS OF ANALYSIS AND EMERGENT PHENOMENA

One can study social and behavioral phenomena at various levels, depending on their nature and the complexity of the units being investigated. For example, sensory psychophysiologists study the neural processes in the visual system that produce the sensory experiences of color, motion, and depth. At a higher level of analysis, psychologists study the complex phenomena of color constancy (the tendency of humans to see the same color, despite the fact that the surface may be reflecting differing amounts of light). At an even more complex level, social anthropologists or linguists study the influence of a culture's language on the richness of its color-naming vocabulary (for example, there are many societies that do not have words for orange, yellow, and green).

Different social scientists interested in the same problems offer different levels of analysis. Thus, psychopathological behavior may be studied by a biopsychologist at the level of factors in the nervous system; by a developmental psychologist as a function of parental handling in infancy; by a sociologist as a result of the impact of social class on the behavior of its members; by a political economist in terms of the cost/benefit of treatment, incarceration, community disruption, and so on.

The levels of analysis—from those concerned with biological phenomena to those concerned with cultural phenomena—form a continuum, ranging from those involving the smallest units to those involving the largest ones: biopsychology to psychology to social psychology to sociology to social and cultural anthropology to economics and politics to ecology.

Historians seek to establish the record of events at almost all of these levels. Their work includes the comparative study of ideas, actions, and lives through biography, archival records, philosophical and scientific treatises, and other traces of human activity, across places and over time, within the framework of history as a social science.

Each level of analysis and description—whether biological, psychological, or sociological—has its own set of laws that can operate without reference to the other levels. Although scientists assume that each set of laws is based on and derived from a set of processes at a more fundamental level of analysis, they nevertheless recognize that such *higher-level processes are emergent phenomena that require study in their own right and require concepts that need not have a parallel with those being used at the lower levels.* As complexity increases, processes and systems acquire new characteristics related to—but not readily extrapolated from—the properties of their more fundamental and less complex components. Thus, vision (for example, the phenomenon of color constancy) is emergent from neural processes in the receptors and brain, but descriptions of these cannot "explain" the resultant visual phenomena. We cannot totally understand the behavior of an individual by reducing it to biological processes; nor can we adequately understand social, political, and economic phenomena by reducing them to the aggregated psychological processes of the participants. For example, it is not possible to explain modern mass warfare by referring to the aggressive tendencies of individuals. Although the laws of economic behavior are believed to be derived from the behaviors of many, many millions of people buying and selling in any particular society, the summed behavior of those individuals cannot totally explain the molar events.

Furthermore, individuals and groups belong to multiple levels and varieties of different systems at the same time, and they behave accordingly. (People behave differently, sometimes dramatically so, depending on whether they are, say, alone, with their family or with peers, with like-sex or other-sex companions, with older or younger persons, or in a crowd.) (See discussion of systems below.)

SYSTEMS

As in the biological sciences, the concept of systems provides a particularly useful and general orienting perspective for the analysis of social and behavioral phenomena. Differing levels of functioning (biological, psychological, interpersonal, cultural, or ecological) can be viewed as composing overlapping and interpenetrating systems, each consisting of parts interacting so as to maintain (1) their own integrity, (2) some form of balance with other parts of their system, and (3) jointly, the integrity of the whole system of which they are a part.

Systems are dynamic. They are demarcated by boundaries (cells by outer membranes, families by biological or legal relationships, regions by geographical borders or spheres of influence, and so on). They vary in degree of specialization and integration of their components, involvement with other systems, and openness to their surroundings. As a consequence of being part of a system, components have properties that they do not have when they are separate from that system or when they function as part of a different system. Thus, it is necessary to study the characteristics and levels of functioning of particular systems to understand their dynamics and predict their behavior.

Organisms can be understood as biopsychological systems maintained by the interplay of biological (neural, physiological, biochemical, etc.) and psychological (perception, cognition, motivation, etc.) processes of integration, which, in turn, interact with the social and physical environments. The concept of human personality—as serving to integrate biopsychological, behavioral, psychosocial, and sociocultural inputs, and helping to organize and determine the individual's responses—describes one such dynamic system within the individual.

Psychosocial systems reflect interactions of individuals and groups (friends, families, peer groups, neighborhoods, organizations, etc.), whereas sociocultural systems, both formal and informal, involve the formation and maintenance of such categories as classes, castes, and cultures. Beyond these, one can examine economic and political systems (including the formal organizational/governmental apparatus of states and nations, trading patterns, etc.), and how these interact to form various international systems. International trade is an example of a dynamic system that interacts with monetary, transportation, and economic systems and subsystems at both sociocultural and regional levels.

Looking at the matter in still another way, one can study cultural interfaces and ecological systems (defined by the interface of living forms and their shared environment, up to and including the biosphere), and the consequences of contacts between societies within cultures and of differing cultures, and the reciprocal effects of the interaction of these with their material (including technological) environments.

A large variety of issues, including those of race, ethnic groups, cultural patterns, and other bases on which individuals, groups, and cultures are differentiated, can be illuminated by examining them from the perspectives of differing system levels (such as individual, family, state, culture, or international community) and types (economic, political, etc.). Such perspectives can also be used to instruct students as to the wide variety of occupational and social roles required for the functioning of an advanced, heterogeneous, technological society.

Additionally, human/machine systems set behavioral requirements for human functioning that are increasingly modifying the nature of interpersonal and social systems (for example, the impact of the automobile on neighborhoods, of automation on the work force, and of telecommunications on the autonomy of individual nation-states). Human engineers design machinery (for example, traffic control signal systems, aircraft and other instrument panels, user-friendly computers, and mechanical arms) to function within the limits of human sensory, motor, and cognitive capabilities. Flexible automated systems enable parts to be exchanged within a manufacturing assembly system in any sequence without having to follow a linear assembly line. Such systems maximize safety, efficiency, and effectiveness; minimize stress; extend the capabilities of both able-bodied people and people with disabilities; and enable organizations to gain economic advantage. Social engineers design work, social, economic, and political environments to achieve certain objectives (for example, worker participant programs to improve job satisfaction, reduce absenteeism, and increase output; and food-stamp programs). The consequences of such changes on social systems—including their traditional hierarchical orderings—have to be anticipated if transitions are to be coped with without system disruption or even disintegration.

The following interrelated concepts help amplify understanding of the dynamics of systems: change, function/malfunction, equilibration/disequilibration, carrying capacity and stress, coping/adaptation, conflict/competition, information and feedback, decision making, trade-off, and resource allocation.

CHANGE

All living systems are more or less open, and therefore cannot be completely stable. The internal heterogeneity of a complex system engenders change within that system; at the same time, the system is developing in relation to its external world. That development may alter the external world or, in turn, be altered by it.

Systems may grow, develop, evolve (expanding in size, becoming more complex, or changing in function), or they may simplify over time, decay, or disintegrate (for example, all living things grow, develop, and die; species arise and evolve, but may also become extinct; empires are established, expand, are transformed, are dismantled, or are destroyed). Systems develop and/or evolve in response to innate programs (for example, genetic blueprints, laws, political constitutions, or equivalent plans; and needs and motives) and in response to external pressures and opportunities (whether demographic, physical, economic, or technological). They tend to alter the conditions that brought them about in the first place and thereby create the possibility of transformations that did not previously exist. Thus, complex political and cultural systems have evolved from pre-existing ones, and existing languages have evolved from earlier forms, in response to changes in the larger environment of which they are part and to which they in turn contribute. Systems may change over time in an orderly and predictable manner (succession); or—given the complexity of simultaneous internal and external relations—systems may change in unexpected, even chaotic ways.

The individual components of a system may change in different ways. They may transfer to or be recruited by another system, cease to function, or lose their identity as parts and give rise to a qualitatively new system. (For example, an individual may graduate from school and enter college, or take a job or transfer from one work situation to another; a person may divorce a spouse, thus leaving a kinship system; a person may marry again, leaving one family to start a new one; in an economic system, the currency may fail and the exchange system revert to barter; and, in a political system, countries can become independent or, conversely, become absorbed by others.

FUNCTION/MALFUNCTION

The structure, organization, and behavior of biological and social systems are logically related to their function and are vulnerable to disruption. Disruption can occur for differing reasons (for example, a sensory system may malfunction due to vitamin deficiencies in the biological structures that generate the neural input or as a result of inadequate or conflicting informational input; an educational system may malfunction because it has insufficient human and material resources for its schools, or its classes are too large to be effective or too small to be economical; and a governmental system may malfunction because it fails to meet the needs of its constituents or because it misallocates its resources).

Often, it is the malfunctioning of a system that motivates people to try to understand how it works and how its normal functioning is achieved. Thus, for example, disease stimulates research to gain the basic knowledge of bodily processes necessary for the development of a cure; crime provides an impetus for the study of the social systems in which it occurs; and war impels attempts to understand the international political system of which it represents a malfunction.

EQUILIBRATION/DISEQUILIBRATION

Systems are said to be in balance, or equilibrated, when the demands upon them are neither too low nor excessive for their carrying capacities or their potential for adaptation (coping). Disequilibration (within and between systems) occurs when components fail to function appropriately or coordinately. There are always tensions between individual components of a system and its overall needs (for example, at the level of politics, between individual decisions and enlightened public participation). In the long run, if needs exceed capacities, or if excess (and costly) capacity continues to be maintained and not utilized, the integrity of a system is jeopardized, and the system is in danger of collapse. Systems may go into wider and wider fluctuations and reequilibrate, or the changes that take place in a system may cross thresholds beyond which the system itself either breaks down or is transformed.

CARRYING CAPACITY AND STRESS

Carrying capacity, or resistance, is the residual, at any given time, of the interaction (trade-off) of a system's resources or strengths and its cumulative experience with stressful input. *When a discrepancy between demand and available carrying capacity exceeds acceptable levels, stress results.* Thus, stress can be due to either an increase in demand or a lessening of carrying capacity. Each system has a different carrying capacity, which can change from time to time. Analysis of the limits of such carrying capacities helps determine a system's vulnerability to stress (and, for example, the resulting physical and mental illness; or economic or political system breakdown). *The carrying capacity of organisms depends upon both inherited biological qualities and cumulative experience, as well as the demand characteristics of the immediate environment.* The carrying capacity of social, economic, and political systems depends on such factors as degree of system integration, control exchange, flexibility, and resource availability.

COPING/ADAPTATION

Systems can reequilibrate by coping with (adapting to) changing circumstances (for example, the development of immunities at the biological level; changing response patterns at the psychological or sociological levels; modifications in political systems at the state level; and the repatterning of modes of economic and political interdependence at the international level). *Systems best survive stressful conditions when they are flexible*—that is, when they can be transformed structurally or functionally by reorganizing, or by incorporating new elements (or replacing or modifying existing ones) to permit the reestablishment of equilibrium, albeit at new levels. In the process of change, disorientation may occur. The presence of anchor points that connect earlier and later conditions facilitates the adaptation process. (A child bringing a favorite toy into a novel environment, for instance, carries an anchor point that helps the child to cope.) If the disorientation is short-term, it creates stress in the individual that can be overcome. If the disorientation is long-term, it represents a form of pathology.

The concept of adaptation does not imply that there is a preexisting fixed environment to which organisms or systems adapt. Within limits, living organisms select their environments and—through their activities—contribute (both favorably and unfavorably) to changes in those environments, changes that in some circumstances may require repeated initiation of new coping strategies. All parts of a system need not respond optimally to changing conditions; nor does change always need to be complete. Sometimes an "unneeded" structure or behavior may take on a new role or may continue to function autonomously (for example, the sheriff system). In other cases, arcane or anachronistic forms remain as inadvertent consequences of system reequilibration (for example, one's appendix, greeting rituals, toasts on drinking, phobic behaviors, and constitutional monarchs). Without knowledge of the history of a system, such structures or behaviors may seem mysterious or inexplicable to students.

Coping in conflict situations can involve the generation of new strategies to achieve collaboration or cooperation. Such strategies may include the use of compromise, coercion (for example, intimidation, domination, or physical violence), or less drastic action to modify the situation, or the use of defense mechanisms (such as rationalization, denial, repression, or attribution) to neutralize the conflict. Most conflict resolution involves cost. The bases for noncoercive resolutions, used by both individuals and groups, range from rationally derived decision schemes that permit evaluation of feasible alternative outcomes to intuition (which may be based on varying amounts of accumulated experience and therefore may not necessarily be irrational).

CONFLICT/COMPETITION

Conflict and competition between the needs of systems, and between their components, is almost inevitable and can result in disequilibration. Conflict occurs when a choice is required between incompatible but equally powerful goals or between incompatible behaviors. It may involve making a choice between mutually exclusive and equally attractive alternatives (for example, two lovers or two careers); equally negative alternatives (for example, war or surrender); or alternatives that have equally powerful positive and negative aspects (for example, a desirable career that requires undesirable relocation). Humans also have multiple concurrent, ongoing roles in social systems (some episodic, some continuous), the requirements of which can result in conflict (such as between the roles of child versus friend versus student; or parent versus spouse versus worker; or individual consumer versus citizen).

Goal incompatibility can occur at all levels, from intrapsychic to international. Conflicts over ownership or control of resources, for instance, may arise between individuals (for example, between neighbors or heirs), individuals and institutions (for example, conflicts involving eminent domain), groups (for example, conflicts over such issues as urban renewal or resettlement), or nations (for example, border, trade, or ideological disputes). Although useful analogies can be drawn, conflicts at the group level (regional, international, etc.) cannot be fully explained through an understanding of either intraindividual or interindividual conflict.

Failure to resolve conflict may result from misconceptions of the need for change, incapacity, or an unwillingness to change (for example, by individuals who have vested interests). For example, tensions can develop in group situations when social configurations and behaviors fail to adapt to changing power patterns in the larger social, political, and economic complexes in which they participate. Such failure, in turn, may lead to states of disequilibration (stress) for the individual (resulting in divorce, breakdown of health, or suicide) and to equivalent conditions (lawsuits, civil disorders, recessions, revolutions, or wars) for organizations, or political entities. In less-than-overwhelming situations, on the other hand, competitive stress can be helpful when it forces a party or parties to seek creative solutions.

INFORMATION AND FEEDBACK

Biological and social systems can preserve stability by acting upon their environments or by reorganizing. Such interactions require integration (coordination) of inputs of information and energy with outputs (behavior) and, via feedback, with the consequences of such outputs.

Information, in the form of relevant signals of change (inputs) from internal and external environments, is used by systems (individuals, groups, or institutions) to maintain their functioning. Relevant signals (information) are distinguished from signals that are irrelevant ("noise") and from redundant signals that do not add to knowledge of the environment even though they reflect it. Incoming information must be interpreted, organized, compared, integrated, and stored with preexisting information (for example, DNA code, memory systems, archives, and libraries); stored information can be retrieved if found necessary for procedures governing output or action.

Feedback across systems and system levels ensures mutual influence (both activating and inhibiting) and is necessary for the coordination of systems (both internally and externally). Systems (for example, the immune system, medical systems, police and legal systems, welfare systems, international trade, and treaty organizations) monitor the functioning of internal components to govern, replace, reconstitute, isolate, or reject those that interfere with their overall functioning (that is, system equilibration).

Such monitoring occurs ordinarily through negative feedback processes. Systems without feedback, or those in which feedback processes fail to operate, are at best inefficient and may be highly vulnerable. Systems with positive or nonlinear feedback can be highly unstable. In the case of nonlinear systems, the consequences of choice, random or even purposeful, cannot be predicted, as each may amplify the dynamic processes, and even the smallest differences can have far-reaching, even chaotic effects (for example, ecological changes, as a result of destruction of the rain forests; and the increasing potential for major war as national governments escalate arms production in response to each other).

DECISION MAKING

Cognitive capacity (including consciousness and the use of written and spoken language) enables humans to analyze problems and make decisions about them. Decision making at all levels is affected by prior systems of values and ethics, cost/benefit ratios, risk (likelihood and seriousness) of the occurrence of unfavorable consequences, degree of ambiguity, reliability and adequacy of available information, and certainty or uncertainty of outcome (the nonlinear and heterogeneous nature of probability).

Much decision making requires predictions to be made in situations that have a large component of inherent uncertainty owing to the complexity of the interrelated and changing factors that determine outcomes. When a series of decisions must be made, individuals and groups may choose to average their decision-making outcomes, seeking a good overall base rate ("batting average") rather than trying to eliminate unique sources of uncertainty in each case (see discussion of trade-off below).

A central problem in the resolution of group conflict is integrating particular opinions, privately arrived at, into group decisions (for example, the processes of group polarization and "groupthink," relevant to the deliberations of juries, the functioning of committees, the work of presidential advisers, and so on). A related difficulty is that of maintaining individual judgment when pressured (overtly or covertly) to subordinate one's own opinion to conform to that of the group norm or to that of the dominant member or members of the group. Conflicts that involve ethical or moral choices can be difficult to resolve on purely objective, quantitative grounds.

TRADE-OFF

Maintenance or restoration of system equilibration can be achieved normally only at a cost. The cost may be the loss of some resource already available or the forfeit of a potential benefit. In such situations, a cost/benefit trade-off (an adaptive response that trades some amount of one kind of benefit for some amount of another) is necessary. An example in nature is the case of animals that forage for prey. There is a cost, in time and energy spent searching, but there is a gain in energy when prey is found and eaten. Search strategies result in different trade-offs (for example, one that never recrosses the same patch of territory is likely to be more efficient for slow-moving prey than one that does, but less advantageous if the prey is swift). Systems survive insofar as they develop efficient trade-off strategies.

The need for trade-offs occurs often, and they frequently have to be made in complex situations (involving overlapping choices) and without certainty of the exact costs and benefits that will accrue in each specific instance. Hence, *the optimal trade-off strategy is likely to be one that is efficient on the average over a series of choices, although not necessarily the most efficient in any particular choice situation.* Some trade-offs involve ethical issues, which may arise when aspects of system survival come into conflict with survival of other (either component or external) units—as, for example, where preservation of "the common" (indivisible rights of all to enjoy resources) comes into conflict with "the noncommon" (privacy or individual ownership).

RESOURCE ALLOCATION

Although many resources (defined as whatever are desired or needed by individuals or groups) seem to be in ample supply, others are limited (either absolutely or in the rate of availability for competing demands). Consequently, resources must be allocated among individuals and groups through either symmetrical and reciprocal or asymmetrical processes of exchange. Examples are recreational time, affection and goods between spouses and parents and children; profit between employers and employees; and energy, space, materials, and wealth between have and have-not nations. Assignments of entitlements and rewards may be made on the basis of merit, need, power, equity, and so forth. Decisions regarding allocation of resources thus may involve issues of relations of political, economic and/or psychological power (in situations involving management versus labor; class; gender—males versus females, etc.).

Humans seek comfort, companionship, entertainment, challenge, jobs, love, money, prestige, and so on, as well as resources essential to maintain and reproduce life. Political and economic systems distribute resources in the form of capital, food, energy, information, labor, land, minerals, shelter, and so on. Cultural values affect definitions of natural resources (for example, the types of goods and services produced; food considered healthful, tasty, disgusting, or taboo; and agricultural, animal husbandry, and food-processing techniques used to produce the food). In addition, the desirability of some resources may change as a function of availability (collector's items, fashion, resort space, living space, etc.).

Amongst all peoples and in all societies, issues of resource allocation involve values and ethics, and require the setting of priorities. A perennial question is whether resources (such as tax dollars, land usage, and communal services) are to be exploited for immediate use by those with access to them; shared with others who lack such access; and/or conserved or replenished for continuing further use by current users or future populations.

SECTION 2

BIOPSYCHOLOGICAL PRINCIPLES AND PROCESSES

The following principles are central to an understanding of evolution, of individual development, and of psychological processes:

- *The genotype of each biological species prepares it to display a particular range of actions or competencies, given certain experiences. Organisms have differing stages of readiness to react at different times, depending upon cyclic and other sensitizing and/or inhibiting factors that may be present at the moment.*

- *There is ordered biological and psychological development, determined both by biological changes and by the nature of social experience.*

- *There is always an interaction between the nature of the organism and the environmental events it encounters.*

EVOLUTION

Natural Selection

The evolutionary theory of the origin of species proposes that species are not immutable; rather, they have evolved as a result of natural selection. For the theory to be understood, the following facts need to be comprehended. First, many more offspring are produced than can survive. Second, there is a struggle for survival by both individuals and groups, including interspecies competition (for necessary resources in limited supply, such as territory and food; and prey/predator ratios) and intraspecies competition (for scarce resources, including sexual partners). Third, species, and individual members of any given species, vary as a result of genetic mutation and of new genetic combinations consequent to sexual reproduction. Fourth, any organism with a variation, however slight, that better enables it to adapt to the complex and varying conditions of its particular environment has a better chance of surviving, compared to its fellows lacking that variation; thus, such a new and modified form will tend to have a reproductive advantage. Fifth, sexual selection (systematic preference for sexual partners possessing certain characteristics over those without them) contributes to hereditary modification of the species, as does imposed selection by a breeder.

The evolution of organic structures can be inferred from the evidence of progressive modification through geological time of the actual remains of such structures (fossils); comparative embryological development; mutual affinities, similarities, and differences amongst species; geographic distribution of variations; mutations; and significant hereditary modifications, as a consequence of imposed selection by breeders of domesticated animals (for example, pigeons, horses, sheep, and dogs) that achieve accumulation of slight variations in a given direction in a set of breeding stock.

The evolution of innate adaptive and social behavior sequences (instincts) is inferred on the basis of probable functions of anatomical remains, cross-species and cross-cultural data (similarities and differences in characteristic behavior of different groups of animals and of peoples—for example, in facial expression of emotion), and studies of artifacts and environmental traces.

It is important that students understand that "fitness" does not mean "good" or "better" in some moral, aesthetic, or "value" sense; rather, it means a fit with a particular set of conditions (for example, the clam "fits" its particular water environment better than a human does).

Humankind

The theory of the evolutionary origin of humankind assumes a link to other animals; it is inferred from finds of fossils and prehistoric tools that can be dated. Humankind's earliest ancestors were not modern apes, which have their own evolutionary history. *Homo erectus*, a species similar to modern mankind, but with a smaller (and presumably less developed) brain, may have appeared as long as 2.5 million years ago. Evidence suggests that our larger brained *Homo sapiens* ancestors emerged some 200,000 years ago.

All species modify their environment in some way, but humans alter theirs far more than any other creature does. Humans are not confined to a narrow environmental niche. Rather, they are capable of planning and carrying out extensive alterations to their environment to adapt it to their own needs. To an extent, much of the environment in which humans now live has been created by them.

With regard to the recurring debate about racial differences among people, evidence suggests that racial differences are minor compared to racial similarities and that all people are part of the same species. Groups of people that are given racial labels are neither discrete nor as different as the idea of species connotes in animals.

HEREDITY AND NURTURE

Heredity

Heredity is a process in which each genotype (the complete genetic endowment of a given individual) is the unique end product of many mechanisms that promote wide ranges of biochemical individuality and genotypic diversity: The interactions of different environments with individual genotypes determine the individual phenotypes (appearance, structure, physiology, and behavior). *What are inherited are not traits but the potential to develop certain traits under certain conditions* (and thus, within limits, differing traits under differing conditions), leading to great diversity among individuals. Psychological traits displayed by individuals are not unitary; most are profoundly affected by many factors, including past learning, present motivation, and state of health.

Human Continuity and Diversity

Many human characteristics are universal. These characteristics include basic biological structures; physiological, sensory, and motor processes; some patterns of emotional expression; and (what is most important) a fundamental plasticity that is based on the remarkable capacity of humans to learn, to develop speech, and, in groups, to generate and sustain a shared culture that is transmitted from generation to generation. Much of the rich diversity in humankind can be attributed to this plasticity.

Psychological processes, including the capacity to learn and to use language, depend on basic biological features of the human brain. Biopsychologists relate findings from the study of the functioning of the nervous and endocrine systems to the understanding of how motivational and emotional states are aroused, sustained, and terminated; how sensation, perception, learning, memory, and action occur and are coordinated; and how damage to the nervous system contributes to behavior pathology.

Language provides the base for culture, which in turn provides guidelines for thought and action. In learning a language, humans unconsciously induce a set of rules governing speech with which they can generate an indefinite number of new verbal communications. By expressing their thoughts in conformity with such rules, they make themselves comprehensible to others who share the same language.

Even the attributes of individuals that appear to be relatively stable (for example, intelligence and certain temperamental or personality traits) are subject to change to the extent to which the environment encourages or discourages their development or maintenance. Agents of socialization (for example, families, peer groups, schools, churches, governments, and the media) transmit shared values, culture, behavior, and expectations that produce greater similarity in children of like backgrounds. Psychologists have developed batteries of tests that are widely used to assess the attributes of individuals by sampling behaviors reflective of them.

Development

Development in normal children is characterized by the regular appearance of a set of universal qualities at particular ages. These qualities include, for example, an enhancement of memory toward the end of the first year, symbolism by the first birthday, speech by the second birthday, the ability to relate concepts and categories by the sixth birthday, and the ability to detect consistency or inconsistency in arguments by adolescence. Development of these increasingly complex levels of intellectual competence is a function both of increasing brain maturity and of appropriate learning experiences, including practice in categorization (see Appendix A). Such development enables children to remember and manipulate more information, infer and deduce more varied ideas, and (what is most important) recognize consistencies and inconsistencies in their beliefs.

Succeeding phases of the life cycle unfold at different rates for different individuals and circumstances. Individual differences in the rate of appearance of these universal dimensions—as well as differences in motives, desires, and standards—are thought to be a function of certain temperamental qualities and differing experiences. The transition from one developmental phase to another is not necessarily smooth, particularly when biological changes are dramatic and/or not in synchrony with changes in social-role expectations and capacities (for example, in the transition from childhood to adolescence and the transition from adolescence to adulthood).

If the environment fails to provide specific kinds of stimulation at the right time, appropriate biological and psychological development may fail to occur. For example, research has shown that infants require "mothering," "nurturing," or "bonding," with affection and protection, to thrive physically and psychologically; peer-group experiences to develop normal social behaviors; and other appropriate early experiences to develop normal functioning, including language.

PSYCHOLOGICAL PROCESSES

Perception

Humans come to know the world through sensory receptors and those areas of the brain that create representations of sensory experiences. The sensory receptors are variously specialized to transform certain classes of physical stimuli (light, chemicals, and pressure) into electrical signals, which are transmitted to the brain. Perception is limited by the range of stimuli to which sense organs respond; although our sensory systems are remarkably finely tuned and have, for their size, enormous dynamic ranges, they respond to only a limited part of the vast array of physical stimuli that impinge on us (for example, the eye is sensitive to only a small fraction of the entire electromagnetic spectrum).

Incoming information is greatly filtered and coded by the sensory system, and the processing involved is complex (that is, it is not a single, linear transformation). Thus, our mental representations (perceptions) of the world are qualitatively very different from the world of physical events that physicists report is "out there" (the hues, tones, tastes, and smells that we perceive are described by physicists as surfaces reflecting electromagnetic waves of certain frequencies; objects vibrating at different frequencies; chemical compounds; etc.). Although this is so, our perceptions nevertheless correspond well with such properties of things as size, form, and location, measured objectively.

The sensory system is particularly sensitive to changes in magnitude and pattern of impinging physical stimuli; it is plausible that the system has evolved as particularly sensitive to those changes that are of significance to the survival of organisms. Members of every species must perceive certain aspects of the external world correctly; if they did not, they could not obtain the necessities of life or avoid its dangers. Motives and emotions have only minor effects on the perception of such properties of objects as size, form, and location; if perceptions were controlled by needs and feelings, they would not provide information of the real world. But experience, motivations, and emotions do influence our interpretations of our perceptions (especially of ambiguous and suggestive stimuli)—and focus our attention on, and make us more sensitive to, the presence of arrays and patterns of stimuli most relevant to our motive and affective states.

Topics of importance in developing an understanding of sensory and perceptual processes include the determinants of attention, sensory discrimination, and individual differences in capacities (for example, acuity and reaction time); the effects of such conditions as sensory deprivation and sensory overload, and of adaptation level in sequential presentation; perceptual constancy; psychophysical measurement; and the distortions and illusions characteristic of sensory systems (the explaining of which challenges perceptual theory).

Cognition

Humans create representations of their experiences. Cognitions are variously described as attitudes, beliefs, concepts, feelings, images, propositions, prototypes, schemas, symbols, thoughts, and so on. Processes of perception and cognition (knowing) involve organization, interpretation, comparison, storage (in different memory systems), and retrieval of mental representations (or cognitive units).

Patterns of cognition are influenced by information presently available, experiences, and ongoing biological and psychological processes (including motivation, expectations, belief systems, attitudes, arousal levels, language, and social factors). Problem solving and creative thinking occur when discrepant events that cannot be understood happen and habitual strategies fail, forcing the development of new conceptual frameworks and/or patterning of ideas, including the use of analogies.

Consciousness

Consciousness is a state of awareness of only a selected portion of the individual's memories, psychological processes, and sensory input. Motor skills (for example, walking, rowing, typing, and other rote processes), once well learned (overlearned), become largely automated, thus permitting a relatively uncluttered consciousness to deal with the demands of immediate circumstances. Unexpected changes in or disruptions of ongoing stimulus patterns restore attentive awareness (vigilance), at least momentarily. Children learn to speak without conscious awareness of grammatical structure or of phonetic or phonemic rules. The concept of the "unconscious" was developed to account for ongoing processes, lying outside immediate awareness, that determine behaviors and experiences. People are unaware of many psychological, social, and cultural influences that affect their lives. Unpleasant memories, or those producing anxiety, may be kept out of consciousness by mechanisms such as repression or denial. Education can be used to increase awareness of unconscious variables and values.

Motivational and Emotional States

Motivational and emotional states, involving physiological and neurochemical as well as psychological arousal processes, are selectively associated with specific classes of deprivation and/or the presence of specific incentives. Behavior patterns can be elicited and sustained by needs (such as sex, thirst, hunger, or safety), goals (achievement, status, etc.), or emotions (such as love, fear, joy, or anger). Levels of arousal, and the persistence of behavior (sustained effort), are affected by the combination of biological processes, such as hormone activity on the one hand and the psychological processes of affective memory and of anticipation of satisfaction or dissatisfaction with the outcome of behavioral effort on the other hand.

Motivation may be intrinsic (satisfaction being derived from behavior itself) or extrinsic (reward-dependent). Individuals differ (with age, sex, personality, temperament, training, and culture) in the relative strengths of components of their motivational profiles; in their ability to delay gratification in order to attain long-term goals; in their ability to enjoy the activity itself (versus extrinsic rewards); and in the role that hedonism plays in their lives.

Learning

Learning may be understood, at least in part, as the way organisms utilize predictive signals of environmental variation to modify their behavior to adapt to changing conditions. Ordinarily, actions that lead to satisfaction and/or fulfillment of expectations (reinforcement) tend to be repeated; those that fail to satisfy or fulfill, or lead to pain or negative emotion (punishment), tend to be avoided. Learning involves the acquisition, modification, retention, and extinction of knowledge (concepts, schemas, scripts, and semantic and lexical distinctions), as well as responses and behavior patterns. It occurs in accordance with principles of associative learning (classical Pavlovian conditioning; and in-strumental or operant conditioning), modeling, and insight learn-ing. Inductive as well as deductive processes are involved in the acquisition of language. The study of learning and memory is informed by both neuroscience and computer science. There is evidence that learning results in differential (task- or situation-specific) physiological and neuroanatomical structural changes in both the developing and the adult mammalian brain (neuro-anatomical plasticity).

Psychological Health/Adjustment

In any given setting, many alternative life-styles can be con-sidered adjusted to a greater or lesser degree. At the same time, a given individual may not be equally adjusted in all areas. Norms of social adjustment and role expectations vary from culture to culture and society to society. They can be broadly or narrowly defined, and can change over time. Beliefs about innate characteristics sometimes shape such norms. In all societies, for example, standards of gender behavior contribute to societal norms of what is considered adjusted (for example, in the Western world, the traditional notion of a correlated set of attributes and behaviors characteristic of each sex has been challenged by evidence that many attributes and behaviors vary independently, so that no single pattern characterizes most men or most women).

Psychological health implies an ongoing dynamic process of biopsychosocial equilibration, functioning, or adjustment, in which environmental demands and individual carrying capacities are proportional to each other.

Psychological and Social Aspects of Biological Health

Psychological stressors (threats, disappointments, demands for major changes of orientation, or behavior to adapt to new situations) interact with the individual's endocrine, immune, visceral, and nervous systems in determining vulnerability to disease. Health habits are affected by psychological and social factors, and they contribute, in turn, to vulnerability to subsequent disease and to compliance with medical treatment. Economic and sociocultural factors and public attitudes affect medical practice, definitions of "illness," etc.

In addition to studying psychological and social factors in disease, research by social and behavioral scientists contributes to the development of psychological techniques for the evaluation and treatment of medical disorders (for example, biofeedback, neuropsychological and psychopharmacological procedures, and behavior modification); to the understanding and management of the psychological and social consequences of medical treatments (for example, use of medications, facing surgery, coming to terms with changes affecting self-image, and living with pain); to the social psychology of the health professions (doctor/patient relationships, physician/nurse roles, etc.); to the development of large-scale public education (social engineering) that is designed to promote better health habits (for example, the use of mass media in antismoking campaigns, periodic breast examinations in women, and alcohol- and drug-abuse education); and to the design, economics, and politics of systems for health delivery and maintenance.

Psychopathology

Behaviors, thoughts, and emotions are likely to be judged as psychopathological when they are sufficiently problematic for the individual or society that the individual becomes dysfunctional—thus requiring some kind of treatment. The diagnosis of psychological malfunction, like that of physical illness, will be uncertain until there are definitive laboratory tests to confirm the clinical judgments involved. In some cases, the diagnosis can be confirmed on the basis of reliable evidence of an underlying biological malfunction; in others, it may be based largely on the degree of deviation from the values and norms of the society in which it occurs. Thus, understanding the etiology of—and treating—disordered behavior requires the application of knowledge of the normal operation of biobehavioral systems and of the social, political, and economic realities of the society in which the behavior occurs.

Psychopathology can be categorized by severity and by symptom clusters. Behavior may be considered neurotic when it impairs—but does not disable—social and psychological functioning. It is considered psychotic when the individual is judged to be manifestly out of touch with reality as others experience it (for example, when the individual exhibits gross disturbances in behavior or thought processes).

Patterns of psychopathology depend on the individual's carrying capacity, determined by predisposing biological factors and psychosocial influences. The latter influences include personality organization, coping patterns, interpersonal social support systems, cultural belief systems, and demographic and economic factors. In some of the most handicapping of mental illnesses, empirical evidence suggests biological involvement (including possible genetic factors). Symptoms of psychopathology usually fluctuate from time to time, sometimes showing complete remission. Although the factors that are associated with improvement and deterioration are as yet unclear, it appears that one such factor is the presence of stress (for example, insoluble personal problems, physical illness, loss of support systems, and exposure to trauma).

There are cultural differences in what constitutes maladjustment. The symptoms of a particular psychopathology may be incapacitating in one environment (for example, to someone trying to survive in a modern urban environment, such as New York City), but much less disruptive in another (for example, to someone living in a less-complex rural area, such as western Kansas). Nor does the appearance of a deviant pattern of behavior automatically warrant the diagnosis of psychopathology, in that such behavior can arise from many other circumstances. When a person behaves in a deviant way in his or her own culture, it may be as an understandable response to circumstances that are not necessarily evident to other people. For example, whereas some mentally ill people express the unfounded conviction that they are the victims of secret persecution, some normal people are actually persecuted. Further, behavior considered psychopathological in one culture may be considered divinely inspired, eccentric, asocial, criminal, or even normal in another. Conversely, when a behavior that is normal in one culture is transplanted into another, very different culture, it can be regarded as deviant (for example, aggressively competitive behavior in a culturally cooperative society).

Specific or generalized mental handicap can result from failure of development or from damage to the central nervous system (variously due to genetic anomalies, traumas, toxins, nutritional deficiencies, hormonal imbalances, stress, etc., that may cause such disorders as fetal alcohol syndrome, Down's syndrome, aphasias, autisms, Alzheimer's disease, and so on).

SOCIOCULTURAL PRINCIPLES AND PROCESSES

SOCIOCULTURAL SYSTEMS

Cultural Development

Sociocultural systems develop with cultural invention and accumulation. They are modified when new patterns (ideas and material traits) are introduced (by way of cultural borrowing and/or diffusion) by migrating groups or through communication and exchange with other cultures (by way of trade, technology, books, the performing and graphic arts, etc.). When traits diffuse into other cultures, they may be blended into traits already existing there and be changed in both form and function (syncretism). The behavioral traits and beliefs that distinguish one culture from another are learned by individuals growing up in those cultures.

Social Attachment

Humans are social animals that ordinarily attach themselves to others. Individuals who experience the loss (death, desertion, or divorce) of their partners or others close to them often suffer depression and an increased incidence of illness; socially isolated individuals may suffer severe psychopathology. Complete detachment from others (and/or place, culture, occupation, or belief systems) is rare.

People—at any one time, and over the course of their lives—belong to a number of social organizations. Membership is determined by biology (for example, biological heritage, sex, or age), happenstance of birth (for example, nationality or class), educational and occupational opportunities, and other individual factors (for example, friendships; and recreational, civic, and special-interest groups). Groups of interacting individuals vary in size and permanence, from temporary assemblages (such as dating couples, audiences, or crowds) to relatively enduring entities (such as married couples, kinship groups, or monarchies). Participants in both may change (and behavior of individuals may change dramatically in some circumstances—for example, crowd behavior).

Modes of Relationship

Modes of relationship between individuals and/or between groups include identification with, attachment to, power over, and subordination to others. Human relationships vary in affective intensity. (Some are passionate, excited, or antagonistic; others are restrained or stoical. In some societies, relationships are warm at home, cool in the workplace; in others, they are cool within families but animated outside.) Relationships vary from nominal to fully merged identity (for example, casual church attenders versus believers) and from follower/supporter to leadership roles (for example, Luxembourg versus the United States as members of NATO).

Types of Exchange of Services and Resources

Types of exchange of services and resources vary within and between groups and contribute to the degree and kinds of satisfaction and/or stress experienced by group members. Exchange patterns include mutualism, with cooperation and equitable reciprocal sharing (of resources, esteem, etc.) between persons, groups, races, nations, etc.; altruism (the sacrifice of self-interest for the welfare of others); competition (striving to win in academic, athletic, economic, social, or political situations); and exploitation (the using of others, on a continuum ranging from ingratiation and minor dependence of individuals or groups on others to slavery).

Social Identities and Expectations

Social relationships, and the roles played by individuals and groups, help determine the views and expectations they have of themselves and of others and the ways in which others view and interact with them (for example, social identities can be structured as components of self-esteem). Such identities and expectations also contribute to the degree to which individuals are tied to their cultures; help determine how people behave, profit from, and contribute (instrumentally and sentimentally) to each other and to the larger social groups and organizations to which they belong; and shape what people expect (for example, recognition, friendship, guidance, or hostility) from others as members of a group or category and as individuals.

Societal norms contribute to values and to what is considered permissible and desirable for the individual to enjoy (for example, family and friendships; accomplishment; power; status; self-fulfillment; spiritual and/or sensual experiences; adventure; work; recreational activities; and creativity) and what is to be avoided (for example, "bad" manners, low grades in school, being fired from a job, irreverence in church, poor grooming, or—at the extreme—incest, and intragroup hostilities).

Expectations of entitlements or availability of rewards (for example, of attainment of "the good life") change as a result of changing demographic, political, and economic factors. In societies with vertical mobility, rising expectations can result from increasing intergroup proximities (actual or inferrable from media presentation; see discussion below of communication). As such expectations, sometimes based on invidious social comparisons, frequently are unrealizable, disappointment and negative affective responses may follow (for example, alienation, aggression, or radicalization). Failure to attain even realistic expectations may result from personal inadequacy, limiting societal or cultural circumstances, and/or changing political and economic realities beyond the control of the individual (such as unemployment, famine, or recession).

Transmission of Normative Values

Individuals learn the normative behaviors and values of their social systems directly (by being taught) or indirectly (by observation and participation). The regulation of behavior (social control) within and between social groups depends on both the desire of members of a society to conform to social norms (that is, individual conscience), and the controls provided by the political and legal systems. Failure in the transmission of cultural values (normally done by way of socialization) may lead to the development of asocial individuals or to the adoption of new social norms. Ambiguity/uncertainty and conflict/ambivalence may result where differing sets of values are transmitted (by parents, the educational system, the church, the entertainment media, peer groups, etc.).

Societal Forms

Societal forms vary in degree of organization and in kind (they are often stratified—sometimes rigidly—and are variously based on age, caste, gender, kin, occupation, politics, race, religion, social class, etc.). The significance of particular societal forms varies from one culture to another, and it can change over time (for example, there has been a worldwide trend for class systems based on exclusive education and special symbolism to become less rigid). Societal forms largely determine access to resources; dominance within territorial/cultural/political complexes; upward/downward mobility of individuals and groups; and patterned belief systems and ritualistic ways of behaving in given circumstances (for example, each culture and subculture prescribes formal sets of behavior at times of birth, death, marriage, and schooling).

Social Stereotyping and Prejudice

Awareness of differences between self (and the groups to which one belongs) and others can lead to social categorization or stereotyping (treating all members of a social category as if they had completely shared characteristics, often based on false generalizations) and to prejudice. Research suggests that simply this awareness of differences—and the opportunity to discriminate—are sufficient to produce in-group preferences. As a consequence, prejudice (negative and positive) is almost inevitable and hard to change, and it often results in imposed limitations or advantages for members of a particular group. Stereotyping, with a sense of entitlements and/or grievances, sometimes results from traditional social and/or political antagonisms and alignments in many parts of the world. In recent years, responses to prejudice have led to widespread identity assertions. This has resulted in improved self-esteem for individuals and attempts at recalculation of what is fair, just, or equitable. At the same time, in many societies, it has contributed to increased political power for leaders of such self-assertive groups, to political and military confrontations, and/or to the rise of separatist movements.

Attitudes based on racial, ethnic, and other stereotyping create complex problems for integration. New groups entering the United

States (always a nation of immigrants), for example, have experienced prejudice in proportion to the threat they represent to existing populations (for example, competition for jobs, resources, and status). Stereotyping is more intense when racial or ethnic identities, cultures, and languages differ; conversely, integration becomes more feasible as goals, values, language, behaviors, and attitudes are shared, even where cultural differences obtain. *Desegregation may be achieved best if it is based on contact between individuals of equal status, with superordinate cooperative goals and institutional support.*

Criminal Behavior

Criminal behavior is defined by the laws of the community in which the behavior occurs. There are various theories of the origins of and the motivations for criminal behavior (for example, financial rewards; limitations of opportunity; criminal socialization; social resentments; and temperamental predisposition to impulsive, aggressive behaviors). Such theories create uncertainty with regard to the appropriateness of various treatments (for example, fines, probation, or imprisonment; and incarceration to effect social isolation versus retribution versus deterrence versus rehabilitation). The Western legal system seeks to evaluate the criminal culpability of an act that breaks a law partly on the basis of whether or not the act was intended; punishment is regarded as immoral except when applied on the basis of the malice of intentions, or "willful ignorance"—hence, "intent" and "free will" are invoked. The concept of "free will" is incongruent with the determinism of much of behavioral science (that is, the view that behavior occurs as an inevitable result of causative factors); and this leads to debate about the appropriateness of punishment for the criminal.

Maladaptive Life-Styles

Individuals differ in the manner and effectiveness of their adjustment in life. While neither outside the law nor considered mentally ill, many individuals develop—or are forced into—lifestyles that are maladaptive for themselves and/or create social problems. Among them are individuals whose behavior and circumstances have negative emotional, social, and economic consequences. Their personalities range from excessively self-seeking or manipulative to ineffectual or reclusive. They may be emotionally unstable, impulsive, excessively restless, borderline in coping capacity, erratic or inadequate in their work performance, have eating disorders such as bulimias and anorexias, be homeless, be irresponsible as sexual partners or parents, and be substance abusers.

Demographics

Both the nature of society and social change are influenced by demographics (age distribution, sex ratios, ethnic origins, racial origins, family sizes and structures, socioeconomic stratifications, percentages of births and deaths, and immigration/emigration patterns; and the economic roles of women, the elderly, etc.).

Demographics, in turn, are influenced by economic, geographical, technological, cultural, and political factors.

The nature of the population in which we live affects how we look to the future and how the future looks to us (for example, is there a sense of open spaces, open opportunities, energy abundance or shortage, and exciting or stagnant cities?). Societies with a stable balance between births and deaths are generally less prone to turbulence; but even in such demographically stable societies, turbulence can exist in pockets of the population or can be controlled by the additional force of political expression or manipulation. Changes in birth-control practices or in life-style, and occurrence of wars and natural catastrophes (for example, famine or pestilence) may dramatically affect the demographic structure of a region or group, requiring significant adjustment and/or reorganization. A "baby boom" implies that if children survive to grow up, they will outnumber and perhaps culturally overwhelm their elders; if it is followed by a decline in birthrate, a society may become top-heavy with elderly people, who may be economically less productive and may require different kinds of resources.

In many traditional, small-scale societies, kin/family tends to be the dominant institution; as societies grow more complex, there is a trend for government and other agencies to play an increasing role in the solution of a variety of problems traditionally handled by kin (for example, educating and socializing children; producing, preparing, and preserving food; caring for the sick, elderly, and severely disabled; providing protection; etc.). The healthy elderly population can be self-sufficient and contribute to the economy through volunteer work and investments without being a burden to either kin or government agencies. The poor and sick elderly, however, do need assistance from others.

COMMUNICATION

Communication requires a sender, a receiver, a signal that bears information from the sender to the receiver, and a channel that carries the signal. Communication can be of aesthetics, cultural norms, directives, emotion, information, values, etc., by way of language and other means (for example, facial expressions, gestures, posture, and bodily movements; and symbolic representations, pictures, or other art forms). Language is a social process; it may be spoken, signed, or written, and it continually evolves to meet new needs for expression and communication.

There are regional, class, occupational, and other differences in both verbal and nonverbal modes of expression. Shared language (verbal and nonverbal) helps generate and maintain a common cultural identity. Literary and artistic communications elaborate, preserve, and perpetuate cultural accomplishments and myths, and humanistic, aesthetic, moral, and ethical values; they provide the individual with enrichment of experiences and the means to express feelings and values. *The constitutional right of freedom of expression protects individual liberty and, in the arts, diversity of tastes across peoples, places, and times.*

In science, openness and exactitude in communication are essential for the sharing of knowledge and for the verification, increase, and effective application of scientific findings. Topics of interest to examine in this particular area include the structure of natural languages; translation; semantics; nonverbal communication ("leakage" of which serves as the basis for lie detection and the transmission of expectancies in experiments, schools, courts, etc.); semiotic systems; artificial languages (logic, mathematics, and computer); and flexibility/precision trade-offs in different languages.

Mass Communication

Mass communication, created by technological advances, has resulted in worldwide transmutation of cultures and the development of modern mass society. Technology provides extended communication capability (direct, worldwide telephone, video, and computer linkage), mass media for information, entertainment, instruction, and persuasion (commercial, political, or religious), and rapid, inexpensive transportation and the interchange of goods and peoples. It is important to understand the role of mass communication in the development of attitudes and the shaping of opinion, in persuasion for political and economic ends, and in disinformation, deception, and distortion.

Visual presentations can be used to give dramatic emphasis to—or to counteract official versions of—events, depending on editing and completeness of presentation (for example, Vietnam War video reports and instant replays). Sometimes, the psychological consequences of media presentations are inadvertent (for example, when emotional adaptation occurs in response to excessive exposure and/or overly insistent presentations). Vicarious experiences (by way of magazines, radio, and television) have come to compensate, for many individuals, for a lack of intimacy in an increasingly impersonal world. Confusion of identity may arise from illusions of intimacy with media "personalities," and may generate false expectations of equality, mutual involvement, and identification with such personalities. Distortions in self-perception and in perceptions of the world at large may result.

Communication technology has also revolutionized the ways in which information can be received, stored, retrieved, and disseminated. It has made possible extended and continuing education and standardized language modeling. Modes of learning and patterns of remembering are being changed as human/machine systems and automated information compilation, retention, and processing are substituted for human efforts of a slower and less efficient (if more personal and internalized) nature. As "external memory" replaces "internal memory," possible serious negative consequences include increased potential for invasion of privacy and less-integrated and more-superficial retention of learned material.

GEOGRAPHY: HUMAN/ENVIRONMENT INTERACTIONS

All places (situations) have distinctive features that give them meaning and character and distinguish them from other places. They can be defined by their locations, or sites; absolutely, in terms of latitude and longitude; or relatively, in relation to sources of energy, water, food, and other basic life-sustaining resources. Places also have distinctive physical characteristics that are derived from geological, hydrological, atmospheric, and biological processes that produce landforms, water bodies, climate, soils, natural vegetation, and animal life. Some places have a very high potential for natural disasters, such as earthquakes, tidal waves, hurricanes, and volcanic eruptions; others—such as areas of intense political unrest, large urban centers, and airport neighborhoods—are vulnerable to human-made disasters.

The impact of human characteristics (ideas and actions) can also be seen in population composition, settlement patterns, types of architecture, kinds of economic and recreational activities, and transportation and communication networks. Also influential in this regard are cultures, ideologies and philosophic or religious tenets, languages, and forms of economic, social, and political organizations.

In addition, places have perceived, or interpreted, characteristics that vary with the experiences and points of view of different observers. Thus, for example, the Central American isthmus is a tropical, mountainous region connecting North and South America; an active volcanic region; a source of tropical agricultural products; a collection of small, independent nations; a region beset with political and social turmoil; a blend of Hispanic and Indian cultures; an example of Third World development in the western hemisphere; or a source of current or potential difficulties in U.S. foreign policy.

All places have advantages and disadvantages for human settlement. For example, high population densities have developed on floodplains, where people could take advantage of fertile soils, water resources, and opportunities for river transportation. By comparison, population densities are low in deserts. Yet floodplains are periodically subject to severe damage, and some desert areas, such as Israel and portions of the U.S. Southwest, have been modified to support large population concentrations.

People both adapt to and modify natural settings in ways consistent with their cultural values, economic and political circumstances, and technological capabilities. Trade-offs occur between competing physical forces and human (and animal and plant) activities as a function of their ever-changing dynamics. Such trade-offs call for counteractive measures that always involve new costs (side effects or consequences) as new benefits are introduced. (See above discussion of trade-off; see also unit below entitled Teaching Notes.)

Movement of goods, persons, ideas, and technologies across places is evidence of—and is used by geographers to measure—global interdependence.

The "region" is a concept used by geographers to define convenient and manageable units for study. Regions are based on selected common characteristics, such as governmental units, language groups, landform types, or types of resource exploitation (for example, the State of Ohio, French Canada, the Andes, or the wheat belt) or a combination of such characteristics (for example, the complex of ethnic, religious, and environmental features that distinguish the Arab world from the rest of the Middle East—and the Amish communities located in Pennsylvania from the rest of that state).

ECONOMICS

Supply and Demand

An economy involves the production, distribution, and use of goods and services. The interaction of supply and demand within an economy determines what goods and services are produced and how and for whom they are produced. Firms and households act as both suppliers and demanders of economic services. Firms demand labor, materials, and capital services as inputs into their production processes, and they in turn supply goods and services. Similarly, households supply labor and capital services (through savings), and they demand the goods and services produced by industry.

Allocations of Goods, Services, and Incomes

Allocations of goods, services, and incomes depend upon tastes, technology, and the availability of resources (work effort, time, land, capital, and so forth) at any given time. *Efficient resource allocation is said to occur when it is impossible to increase the output of any one good without decreasing that of another, or when it is impossible to increase the welfare of any given consumer without reducing that of another* (see above discussion of resource allocation in Section 1).

Maximization

Maximization of consumers' welfare, firms' profits, and the social welfare of society (broadly construed) is the goal of economic decision making in the face of limits to resources. Constrained maximization recognizes that consumers and firms must adapt to resource, budget, and technological constraints. Trade-offs between various alternatives require the allocation of resources on the parts of households, firms, public and private agencies, and governments in such a way that the goals of the particular economic agents (utility for households; profits for firms; social welfare for government; and so on) will be maximized in the context of the existing institutional and resource constraints.

It is important to note, however, that *an efficient allocation of resources may not be consistent with society's views of social justice or equity.* For example, if one factor of production (such as capital) is scarce relative to another (such as labor), an efficient equilibrium may be incompatible with distributional equity or justice. In this case, society may be willing or required to sacrifice some efficiency for social justice (for example, minimum-wage laws). On the other hand, in the presence of such factors as external economies or diseconomies, natural monopolies, limited public goods, or imperfect information, societal intervention may be needed to ensure that the allocation of resources is efficient as well as equitable. An example of such interventions includes the regulation of trade and labor relations.

The Form of the Economy

The form of the economy is related to the social and political history and structure of a society. Alternative economic systems have different approaches to the allocation of resources. *Notions of economic efficiency, distributional equity, and social welfare are not immutable but depend upon the economic system under which a given society operates.* Pure capitalism offers the market solution; pure socialism offers the state—or planned, nonmarket—solution; and mixed systems—which is what all actual systems are—offer combinations of the two.

Economics and Politics

In general, the behavior of economic institutions is closely and reciprocally linked to political institutions; the modern corporation, government, labor and unions, and the military all play different and changing roles, depending upon the nature of the political and social structure.

Cyclical and Secular Changes

Cyclical and secular changes affect economies in the modern world. Economies are never static. Cyclical changes occur in the presence of short-run disequilibria under which markets do not clear (that is, not all offerings are purchased) at current prices. In the case of inflation, demand shocks may cause aggregate demand to exceed aggregate supply, leading to price increases; and supply shocks may create shortages that likewise push prices up. In the case of recession, aggregate supply tends to outstrip aggregate demand, leading to unemployment and to excess capacity in the presence of price rigidities.

Secular changes occur through the development process in less-developed countries and through productivity growth and technical change in developed countries. The transformation from preindustrialized to industrialized society is related to the transformation from a nonmarket to a market economy, the determinants of growth (population, savings, and investment), technology transfer, and so forth. The growth of industrialized societies depends upon productivity increase, the rate of technical change and innovation, savings, and similar factors.

In the case of both cyclical and secular changes, the relationship of a particular economy to the broader economic system is important. The greater the connectedness of an economy to its trading partners, the more it is subject to the cyclical and secular changes of those trading partners.

POLITICS

Functions of Government

Governments are instruments for the authoritative allocation of values and power in a society. The functions of government are instrumental (regulating public order; and providing social welfare, education, communication, transportation, legal and monetary systems, protection, defense, etc.) and value-expressive (providing citizens with a means of common identity and expression). Governments derive their legitimacy (citizens' loyalty) from the fulfillment of both sets of functions.

Structures of Political Systems

Structures of political systems determine the nature of the authoritative decision-making process, the degree of access to it for individual citizens, the claims of the government over spheres of individuals' lives, etc. Political systems vary markedly in their provisions for handling political conflict, citizen participation, degree of concentration of governmental and administrative authority, and the way power is transferred (for example, through kinship, coups, selection by an elite, or elections). Democracies vary among themselves (for example, in form of election of leadership and in amount and role of bureaucracy), and differ even more from authoritarian (whether military, patrimonial, theocratic, one-party, etc.) and totalitarian (fascist or communist) systems.

Political Cultures

Political cultures are defined by their orientations toward political action—including values, ideologies, and rules of behavior (for example, subject versus participant political cultures, trust in government, political identity, patterns of partisanship, and notions of civic obligation). Some political cultures are homogeneous; others are heterogeneous. Within societies, distinct political cultures often exist among different castes, tribes, linguistic and ethnic groups, etc. In many places, there appears to be a close relationship between religion and political culture (for example, Muslim, Buddhist, Hindu, Jewish, Protestant, and Catholic cultures).

Inputs to the Political Process

Inputs to the political process include political socialization and recruitment, interest articulation, and interest aggregation. Political systems vary in the relative importance of different agents of political socialization (for example, family, schools, peer groups, and mass media) and in how (and which) people are recruited into politics and administration. Interest articulation involves the role of public opinion in a polity, and various forms of political participation (varying from seeking information about the political sphere to voting, campaigning, and contacting public officials, and even to engaging in bribery and protest activities). The types and frequency of participation are determined by individual propensities to participate, as well as by institutional incentives and constraints. Political interest aggregation occurs through mediating groups (ethnic, regional, religious, anomic, issue-related, etc.), organizations (for example, political parties and forums), and/or (charismatic) leaders.

Outputs of the Political Process

Outputs of the political process must be analyzed in many ways, including general, long-term policy positions; specific policies; and policy implementation. Political systems differ in the degree to which they ensure their citizens' civil liberties. They also differ with respect to the relation between government and the economy (as, for example, the role of government in the distribution and redistribution of income and wealth, the control and regulation of the means of production, and the facilitating of economic growth). Although doing so is not their exclusive province, governments use mass media and regulatory systems (for example, educational and criminal justice systems) to define and control citizens' behavior.

INTERNATIONAL POLITICS

The International Environment

The international environment must be taken into account increasingly by all governments in conducting their affairs. This environment includes not only other governments but also international systems that have developed as complex functions of the distribution, use, and exchange of human and natural resources. The definition of "national power" has been expanded to recognize the importance of economic factors, including natural resources and changing technological capability, as keys to power status—as, for example, in the cases of Japan and the newly industrializing countries (NICs). Technological sophistication has become a defining feature in current concepts of dependence, independence, and interdependence.

National Goals

National goals in international relations include power (political, economic, or military); self-aggrandizement (imperialism); self-preservation, self-protection, and/or self-determination; ideology; support or imposition of values; attainment or maintenance of justice; proselytizing or maintaining freedom of religion (including rejection or persecution of nonbelievers or heretics); maintenance of identity of ethnicity and culture; and acquisition or preservation of resources (food, energy, knowledge, ideas, technical competence, etc.).

International Systems

International systems include global organizations (such as the United Nations and its agencies and the World Court) and international subsystems, both formal (for example, the European Economic Community, the Arab League, and NATO) and informal (for example, Iberia, and the combination of eastern Canada and the United States). The maintenance of informal international norms ("international regimes") is an important function of both multilateral and bilateral key international partnerships. International systems, unlike national governments, often have loosely defined boundaries and limited authority over their component members (for example, the refusal of the United States to accept the World Court's decision on the mining of Nicaragua's harbors, and the inability of the U.N. Security Council to obtain compliance with its resolutions).

Nongovernmental Transnational Actors

Nongovernmental transnational actors of significance are economic (for example, multinationals, including those of the Third World; labor unions; and central banks), religious (Roman Catholicism, Islam, Judaism, etc.), environmental (for example, Greenpeace), and others (for example, concerned scientists involved in war/peace issues; Amnesty International; the Club of Rome; participants in international sports events, such as the Olympics; international exchanges, such as Fulbright Fellows and Rhodes Scholars; and folk/rock music groups).

Instruments of International Relations

Instruments of international relations include diplomatic communication, trade and finance (conflict, cooperation, and international management), information (generation, transmission, and suppression), disinformation (deliberate deception and propaganda), covert activity, peace and war (nuclear deterrence, conventional warfare, and terrorism), international law, education, treaties, aid, balance of power, and negotiation.

THE HISTORICAL PERSPECTIVE

N *either retrospective nor prospective events can be interpreted entirely in terms of the present* (for example, historical actors lack information that a later reviewer may have: Custer did not know that Sitting Bull was waiting on the other side of the hill—but we do. Likewise, students in the year 2061 will know if the nuclear standoff of the last third of the twentieth century was effective in maintaining superpower peace—whereas we cannot know). Cultural, economic, geographic, physical, political, psychological, sociological, and technological conditions of a particular period of time and locale constraints on what was—and is— possible for the individual and for society. Any given culture depends on many things that may not be permanent or, at best, may be cyclical (such as fossil fuel, normal cycles of climate, food supplies, or conditions of peace). Furthermore, it is difficult to predict with any degree of accuracy the continuing and complex consequences of change, whether they are natural or human-made, accidental or planned.

SOCIAL CHANGE AND CONTINUITY

Some changes are cyclic, and others are ongoing. Historical events can result in irreversible transformations of the cultures in which they occur. These transformations include wars; famines; plagues; new technologies; new geomorphological patterns; new ways of managing resources; new economic, political, or social arrangements; and/or new intellectual, scientific, or religious interpretations of the past or present.

Some transformations have been dramatic, such as those consequent on the development of the printing press, global explorations in the sixteenth and seventeenth centuries, and the more recent impact of the computer and of biotechnology. Other changes that have impact but occur slowly, during the lifetime of the observer, may seem less dramatic (for example, the sequence of changes over time in the length of various phases of the life cycle, such as the extension of adolescence in recent times). Technology (for example, safe, convenient, and effective contraceptives) and changing economic and cultural conditions have resulted in the redefinition of women's political, economic, and social roles vis-à-vis men, which has led to changing popular attitudes about sex, marriage, parenting, and career roles; these attitudes, in turn, may have profound consequences on social organization and culture.

Some changes contribute to the loss of important species of flora and fauna (including even peoples), the transformation of climates and landscapes, and both the loss of cultures and the creation of new ones. Some changes have been beneficial and some have not. Sometimes, whether a change is considered to be beneficial or detrimental depends on one's point of view, which may differ on the basis of the time of its occurrence versus when it is seen from a historical perspective (for example, the

Treaty of Versailles, following World War I, intended to end wars, was later seen as contributing to World War II). Other changes—with consequences for improved health, political freedom, and intellectual and personal development—have clearly bettered the human condition (yet even here, potentially negative side effects and consequences may require that trade-offs and compromises be made).

Emphasis on change should not obscure the importance of continuities. Throughout recorded history, humans have formed social groupings for mutual support and protection and for procreation and the rearing of young; have met challenges with social and technological innovations; and have valued discovery and achievement, creativity and aesthetics, fellowship and family, and an ethical basis for civilized behavior. Religion, with its moral values, has been one of the enduring institutions, even in allegedly secular societies. At the same time, many problem areas have existed over centuries (for example, those created by the existence of disease and mental and physical disabilities; conflicts of interest between individuals and communities over the distribution of resources; power struggles—including wars—among persons, groups, and nations over territory, religious beliefs, etc.).

Finally, one may note that the histories of science and technology, and even of history, have their own histories, which have changed over time. Any attempt to comprehend these larger changes must take into account the ways in which our understanding of the physical and human worlds have changed.

TEACHING NOTES

Historical inquiry can illuminate the complex ways in which economic, social, political, psychological, technological, and environmental forces are integrated in given events or chains of events in the past. A variety of typical clusters of interactions can be characterized (such as industrialization, nationalism, professionalization, and urbanization), and the complexity of cultural systems and the multivariate causation affecting their rise and decline can be portrayed, along with the intellectual, cultural, political, and technological legacy inherited from them. The longitudinal and horizontal study of examples drawn from the following genres can be instructive:

Great Civilizations

Many ancient civilizations (in Egypt, Mesopotamia, Asia, Greece, India, Central and South America, Africa, etc.) have documented histories covering great extensions of their culture in time and space. The study of any of these civilizations provides a background for understanding the influence of ancient belief systems in structuring perceptions of and contributing to the progression of events. Some ancient aspirations and historic enmities—including socially transmitted feelings of inherited guilt, grievance, and entitlement—have continued to play important roles in the political, cultural, and economic conduct of contemporary societies throughout the world—thereby contributing to the maintenance of belief systems and, in turn, being maintained by those systems.

Major Intellectual and Psychological Transformations in Western Culture

Such transformations include the change from tribal religious cults to major moral and ethical systems (Zoroastrianism, Buddhism, Judaism, and Christianity); the importance of Greek and Roman intellectual heritage (Roman law, Greek and Roman philosophy, etc.) in forming the basis of Western civilization and consciousness; and the impact of the Renaissance, the Enlightenment, and the Protestant Reformation on the emergence of the scientific outlook, which itself has changed over the past 400 years.

In more recent times, the expanded development of science and the Industrial Revolution have contributed to the rise of secular belief systems (for example, Marxism, psychoanalysis, and social Darwinism). These systems epitomized the nineteenth- and early-twentieth-century Western belief in progress, with its expectation that all non-Western societies must recapitulate the Western process of development. *Much of Western culture, in which technological innovations have played a massive role, was shaped by belief systems that assigned meanings and values to interpretations of progression of events in time. In contrast, some Eastern cultures created and were shaped by belief systems that emphasize the repetition and the cyclical nature of events.* Both views have come under critical scrutiny. With the increasing intermixture of cultures, it is important that students be given the opportunity to examine the similarities and differences in outlook and consequences for the future of the respective values of Eastern and Western cultures.

One peculiar feature of Western civilization was the unusual level of development of slavery and the effects this had not only on its economic and cultural development but also on many aspects of intellectual life. Greece and Rome were the first civilizations to depend heavily on slaves for the performance of the most advanced economic sectors. It is probable that the idea of freedom—so important in Western intellectual thought—emerged as a central value in ancient Greece largely in reaction to the presence of slavery and the recognition of its spiritual horror and the value of its negation (see discussion below of major economic transformations).

Revolutionary Change

Although political revolutions (for example, the French, American, Russian, and Chinese) vary with the contexts in which they occur, there is a cluster of events they have in common. These events include rapid and accelerated change (social, political, economic, and religious), phases of intensity in social upheaval, challenges to authority (in social institutions varying in scale from the unit of the family—through church, community, work organization and profession—to the state and public authority); trade-offs of freedom and control; changes in manners and codes of morality; and even postrevolutionary "adjustments" (counterre-volutionary phase).

The Rise of Nationalism

Nationalism has resulted from a complexity of economic, po-litical, cultural, psychological, and technological factors. Exam-ples include European state building, from the sixteenth to the nineteenth centuries; nations of settlement (for example, the United States, Canada, and Australia); successor nations follow-ing the breakup of empires (for example, Austria, Hungary, India, and Brazil); and twentieth-century states that give political expres-sion to the aspirations of specific religious and ethnic communities (for example, Ireland, Israel, Pakistan, and the Arab states).

Technological and Information Revolutions

Such revolutions continue to change relations among peoples. Their impact on the international system, in the late twentieth century, can be illustrated by the manner in which multinational corporations and other organizations have used technology to harness resources more efficiently and to maintain lines of communication and transportation among widely dispersed lo-cations. Such changes, in turn, have facilitated contacts across frontiers at all levels and have diminished reliance on central governments as the primary source of information and action.

Technology may have made large-scale conventional war less likely, for fear of escalation to nuclear war (deterrence), whereas, at another level, it has provided a means for the empowerment of new groups and the development of new forms of conflict (remote-control weaponry, plastic explosives, and terrorism). Technology and information exchange have also changed the classifications of issues, blurring divisions among political, eco-nomic, and security questions. Formerly, international relations typically embraced "high politics" (diplomacy and security); today, they increasingly encompass "low politics" (economics, welfare questions, and environmental concerns). Further, high technology and information exchange have become commodities of international relations, with implications for trade, culture, and political, economic, and social development at home and abroad.

Major Economic Transformations

Cultural and political systems, and the nature of individual daily lives, continue to be modified significantly as a consequence of major economic transformations. These transformations have included the discovery and development of agriculture and animal husbandry by early humans with tribal social organiza-tion; the development of feudalism, with its stratified class society; the transition from feudalism to capitalism and a market economy, and the relationship of the latter to the high rate of technological development and expansion of European powers in the Age of Discovery in the seventeenth and eighteenth centuries.

The role of the colonial exploitation of peoples and of various forms of personal domination in the transformation of the West also must be recognized. Slavery, for example, played a pivotal role at key points of transformation of the West—classical Greece, late republican and imperial Rome, in the Italian commercial system of the late Middle Ages, and in the rise of capitalism and settlement of the New World.

Human/Environment Interactions

Human/environment interactions can be seen in the ways in which the same geographic locations have differing successive uses. So, for example, centuries ago, Pueblo Indians developed agricultural villages that still endure in the deserts of the Southwest. Later, Hispanic and Anglo settlers established mineral industries, cattle ranches, and farms in the same desert areas, relying increasingly on the large-scale manipulation of water resources. Still later, perceiving the availability of clear skies, sunshine, and open spaces, people developed resort, retirement, military, and research facilities in the same areas.

Trade-offs between physical forces and human activities can also be seen over time. In coastal California, for example, winter rains and severe erosion from adjacent hills (resulting from forest fire destruction of ground cover) cause flooding and mud slides; the response of building costly dams and sediment traps has reduced damage but has produced side effects such as reduction of beaches and increased rate of sea cliff erosion, resulting in new property losses, the need for costly hauling of sand, etc.

SECTION 5

QUESTIONS OF GOOD AND EVIL

In the beginning and in the end, the social and behavioral sciences must inform questions of good and evil. No other issues are as important. Throughout recorded history, there has been displayed a seemingly endless capacity for "man's inhumanity to man," a refinement of the means of its delivery (often in unbelievably extreme form), and the rationalization of such inhumanity in political, religious, economic, and even scientific terms. On the other hand, paralleling this continuing evil, there has been the development of a series of sublime concepts of love and compassion for life and living beings, and of the means of securing greater likelihood of survival and satisfaction ("the good life") for more people on earth.

The sciences (and scientists) are—theoretically—value-free. Nevertheless, it is self-evident that science and technology—including the social and behavioral sciences and their applications—can be used in negative ways to promote degradation and destruction of human life, cultures, and societies. The power of science applied in these ways seems almost boundless. It should be equally self-evident that the sciences can and should be used to inform such important objectives as the pursuit of peace, ecological balance, compassion, justice, and human freedom, dignity, and welfare. It obviously is vital that they do so.

As part of their instruction in the social and behavioral sciences, students should be helped to recognize—and to appreciate the subtleties of—the moral and ethical implications and consequences of different courses of action or inaction. They also should be taught the use of scientific methods of analysis as a means of illuminating the dilemmas involved in attempting such determinations (see Appendix A).

Although a society cannot ensure that its science is or will be used for good, it can encourage such use by heightening its members' awareness of the issues involved in determining what constitutes "good." Is "good" pleasure? Happiness? Health? Riches? Security? Any or all of these? If we must choose amongst these "goods," which is/are better? And, when we say "good," for whom do we mean it is good? Ourselves? Our children? Our friends? Our nation? Society? Humanity? The environment? Do we mean "good" for now or for the future? For the next generation? The next century? And so on.

Similar questions need to be raised about "evil" (Is it poverty? Economic exploitation? Wanton environmental exploitation? Physical cruelty? Hopelessness? Certainly, it includes slavery, torture, murder, and genocide). In all instances, we must determine whether we are dealing with absolutes or with matters of degree—that is, whether the choices to be made are mutually exclusive; whether the consequences of our choices are temporary or permanent, reversible or not—Can we successfully play zero-sum games?

An essential good is the fundamental capacity of humans to perceive and create patterns, to identify and solve problems, and to engage their environments constructively. Such capacities vary among individuals, and are sometimes engaged serendipitously, but—in virtually all cases—they can be enhanced (or inhibited) through appropriate social and cultural encouragement (or discouragement). While in itself "good," such capacity evidently can serve good or evil ends.

It should be emphasized that good and evil are not always clearly defined polarities. A disturbing feature of moral history is the fact that on one hand, good intentions and deeds often have evil consequences and, on the other hand, often "out of evil cometh good." Further, it is sometimes true that the values and ideals we cherish not only emerged as the unforeseen and unintended consequences of evil acts but continue to maintain a dialectical relationship with their opposites. A case in point is the value of freedom and its idealization in the West, which came about largely as a counterresponse to the West's unusual dependence on large-scale slavery during its years of economic development.

The hardest problem the student must confront is to recognize the nature of the dilemmas involved in issues of values, goals, and ethics, and the difficulty of finding universally acceptable or satisfactory answers to them. For example, inflicting pain or suffering on others (punishment or torture) to benefit oneself may be considered evil; this is not so if the benefit is presumed to be to the individual upon whom the pain or suffering is inflicted (as in surgery). However, the issues are not as clear in cases of mercy killing or extensive and expensive surgery for the hopelessly malformed when a large segment of the population is unable to obtain medical treatment. Such issues present dilemmas because, at first blush, there appears to be no natural base from which to resolve them—no interest that has self-evident priority in guiding decisions. However, this is not entirely true.

Some answers clearly are better than others. For example, the value and quality of individual human life are widely held criteria in assigning relative importance to a moral standard. David Hume, an eighteenth-century philosopher, correctly hypothesized that human beings are capable of empathy with the pain and discomfort of another, and this empathy tends to lead to inhibition of aggression toward others. There now are data from developmental studies showing that children empathize with the pain of another beginning in the second year of life. Such data can help provide the natural base from which one can begin to construct a universal morality.

Understanding might be further advanced by examining and debating the ways in which philosophers, poets, essayists, scientists, and other thinkers have sought—over the centuries—to pose questions about such issues and to answer them, and the extent to which their answers, correctly or incorrectly, may have shaped their civilizations. Such discussion, enriched by the insights to be gained from the systematic approach of modern social and behavioral sciences, can help provide perspective on questions of good and evil as they will continue to confound students and scientists alike in the year 2061 and beyond.

TEACHING NOTES: GOOD AND EVIL

Historic events and their precedents and consequences can provide meaningful study modules to aid students in understanding how good and evil may have emerged and been perpetuated, and the ethical issues and dilemmas they present.

Good

It can be instructive to examine those things that are considered good in our society and how they came to be so considered: rights such as freedom of speech and of religion, universal education and literacy, decent living and working conditions, health care, protection against physical and legal abuse and exploitation, and responsibilities to and for others. One might further examine the historic tendencies (as noted above) of people in virtually all periods of the world's history to create and preserve beauty, to pass along their culture to successive generations, to preserve and protect human life, and to care for their own and also for those in need.

One can look at the watershed conditions that gave rise to such concepts as "inalienable rights" and communal responsibilities, and to the ways in which such values become and remain parts of the structure of a society. A civics lesson—in the form of a discussion of the overall system created by the Constitution of the United States and its amendments, the trade-offs their adoption required, and what life might be like without such provisions and protections—would be a meaningful way to approach such issues.

Other lessons could be designed around the cross-national development of agencies—such as the Red Cross, Oxfam, Amnesty International, and CARE—to aid victims of disaster. Lessons could also be designed around the development of legislation involving child labor and civil rights, and economic aid to former enemies (for example, the Marshall Plan).

Evil

Study modules also can be developed to examine the problem of evil. One such module could be developed around historical examples of massive inhumanity in which—allegedly justified by scientific, religious, or political ideologies—enormous numbers of innocent persons within a culture were systematically persecuted, tortured, and killed in organized attempts to eliminate them. Three such examples are as follows:

● The Inquisition (throughout Europe, beginning in the Middle Ages), with its accompanying trials and executions for heresy, and the related witchcraft trials (which lasted into the eighteenth century, and occurred in the British Isles, elsewhere in Europe, and New England).

● The large-scale program of euthanasia and genocide carried out by the Nazi government of the Third Reich in the first half of the twentieth century, victimizing especially the Jewish population of Germany and its conquered countries but also including physically and mentally disabled people, political dissidents, homosexuals, Gypsies, slaves, and others.

• The Stalinist terror, instituted to eliminate the kulaks and political dissidents in the Soviet Union, in the first half of the twentieth century.

Each of these examples of inhumanity was motivated by ideological beliefs, often with an accompanying sense of self-righteous mission on the part of those who victimized others, and took place in a general climate of fear. In each, the victims were conceptualized as a threat to the welfare of the victimizers. In the first example, the victims were said to endanger the well-being and salvation of souls; in the second, the genetic quality of the human species; in the third, the political and economic fabric of a developing new society.

Attention should also be given to adjunct factors, such as the self-perpetuating character of bureaucracies set up to implement persecution; economic considerations (for example, financial greed, as manifested in the confiscation of property of the victims); the neutralization of opposition by threat or fear; and a permissive climate for individual psychopathology (for example, sadism).

Examples of source materials on the Inquisition and heresy trials include the following:

• Trevor-Roper, H. R. 1967. *The European Witch-Craze of the 16th and 17th Centuries.* Harmondsworth: Penguin Books. (Trevor-Roper analyzed the craze "as the social consequence of renewed ideological war with the accompanying climate of fear" [p. 67].)

• Cohn, N. 1975. *Europe's Inner Demons.* New York: Basic Books. (Cohn concluded that "financial greed and conscious sadism, though by no means lacking in all cases, did not supply the main driving force: that was supplied by religious zeal. The great witchhunt can in fact be taken as a supreme example of a massive killing of innocent people by a bureaucracy acting in accordance with beliefs, which unknown or rejected in earlier centuries had come to be taken for granted as self-evident truths" [pp. 254–55].)

• Boyer, P., and S. Nissenbaum. 1974. *Salem Possessed: The Social Origins of Witchcraft.* Cambridge, Mass.: Harvard University Press.

Source materials on the mass exterminations perpetrated by the Nazi government of the Third Reich include the following.

• Lifton, R. J. 1987. *The Nazi Doctors: Medical Killing and the Psychology of Genocide.* New York: Basic Books. (Lifton described how members of the medical profession, among others, believed that in the interest of the collective society as a whole, they had not only the right but also the responsibility to impose death on "life unworthy of life." That is, they had the right and responsibility to improve the biological future of the human race. They started with coercive sterilization and the euthanasia of disabled babies and children, and later of disabled adults. They then proceeded to attempt mass extermination of entire ethnic groups. Lifton described how the exterminations were viewed not as murder, but as a therapy for the Nordic race by ridding it of so-called undesirable genetic material. He advanced psychological concepts to explain how human beings consent to behave in ways at variance with a previously accepted moral code.)

A major source for the Stalinist use of terror is the following three-volume work, which covers the period from 1918 to 1956: Solzhenitsyn, A. I. 1978. *The Gulag Archipelago*. Harper & Row.

The above source materials can be supplemented by experimental evidence that individuals are able to justify actions that cause pain to others by dehumanizing the victims, by considering themselves to be the agent of others, and by believing that their actions serve the purposes of religion, science, or politics,[1] or by fear and diffusion of responsibility.[2]

The presentation can be amplified by studies of the psychological sequelae (that is, posttraumatic stress syndrome) of survivors of torture and other human-made traumata (for example, the shell shock suffered by soldiers exposed to long periods in the trenches in World War I; and the inability of Vietnam veterans to integrate their war experiences into their postwar lives), as well as of environmental catastrophes (floods, etc.).

Additional study modules can be developed around contemporary examples of uses of torture, terrorism, and genocide by government and antigovernment forces in politically troubled areas of the world (for example, the Central and South American "death squads," and apartheid in South Africa).

Another study module can be developed around the theme of slavery—the ownership of humans by other humans for the purpose of exploiting their labor. The study of slavery highlights the evil inherent in exploitation of humans by their fellows. It is also important to examine this phenomenon in a broad historical context. It is possible that the widespread institution of slavery in the history of the Western world played a pivotal role in the key points of transformation of the West (see the discussion of major economic transformations, in Section 4) and contributed to the importance of the value of freedom in the Western world (see the discussion of major intellectual and psychological transformations in Western culture, in Section 4; and the discussion of questions of good and evil, in Section 5). The very idea of freedom is still most commonly conceived of and expressed, not in positive terms but as the absence of slavery or personal constraint.[3]

Other study modules could be developed on the treatment of American Indians by whites, of Armenians by the Turks, of Koreans and Manchurians by the Japanese, etc.

It is important to provide opportunities for students to recognize that the above examples are not just historic anomalies. Study of the underlying causes makes it clear that the danger of reoccurrence of such evil events is present in modern societies that do not remain vigilant.

---

[1] See, for example, the experimental studies reported in the following work: Milgram, S. *Obedience to Authority*. 1974. Harper & Row.

[2] See, for example, Latan, B., and J. M. Darley. 1970. *The Unresponsive Bystander: Why Doesn't He Help?* New York: Appleton-Century-Crofts.

[3] See Patterson, O. 1982. *Slavery and Social Death: A Comparative Study*. Cambridge, Mass.: Harvard University Press. See also Harding, V. 1981. *There is a River*. New York: Random House/Vantage.

THE SCIENTIFIC STUDY OF SOCIAL AND BEHAVIORAL PHENOMENA

We and the human systems that we create are the subject of study of the social and behavioral sciences. As one examines oneself and one's social setting, it is especially important to distinguish the outcomes possible from applying a systematic, scientific approach from the conclusions that might otherwise be drawn from various common-sense observations in which we might casually engage. Although students may make this distinction easily within areas of the physical sciences, it is essential that they recognize the critical importance of the scientific approach in the study of human nature and human systems. To that end, a brief review of the important aspects of scientific study of social and behavioral phenomena follows.

THE SCIENTIFIC APPROACH

The scientific approach to understanding differs from that based on common sense by following strict rules of inquiry, including the use of careful empirical observations and the explicit formulation of hypotheses and theories designed both to account for the observations and to predict phenomena and relations not previously observed and further empirical investigations planned to assess the validity of such hypotheses or theories.

Attempts to apply scientific methods to the solution of real problems require continuing alertness to—and careful definition of—the nature of the problems (both existing and prospective), as well as recognition of the constraints within which solutions must fall. It is necessary to know where to go for relevant information; how to generate information when it is lacking; how to assess short- and long-term costs, benefits, and risks consequent on each of the possible solutions; and how to resolve conflicts between ethical, psychological, and social (as well as physical and financial) options. (This need holds true whether applied to such settings as home, workplace, or community or to more complex situations, including organizational and governmental management and international relations.)

Problem solving always involves uncertainty, which occurs to the extent that the phenomena involved are a function of chance or of situational or subject variables that cannot be controlled; information, on which predictions of outcomes can be based, is not available or adequate at the time action is required; solutions to one set of problems, in turn, generate new ones; and/or solutions satisfactory to one constituency create problems for other constituencies. Thus, scientific conclusions and predictions are always conceived in probabilistic terms.

Mark Twain commented that "supposing is good, finding out is better." Scientists usually begin by supposing—that is, by formulating hypotheses (explanations, or tentative answers to their questions) based on prior knowledge and theory. Then they find out by undertaking research to determine whether a chosen hypothesis is better than available alternative hypotheses. Their findings generate new hypotheses and stimulate further research. *Science is knowledge based on accumulating evidence, its interpretation, and the further testing of interpretations, with revisions of theories as new evidence warrants.*

In some respects, scientific investigation can be likened to solving a complex puzzle or a whodunit, in which pieces or clues (evidence, observations, or data) are fitted together to arrive at a plausible solution (explanation or theory). Anyone who works on puzzles or mysteries will recognize the many errors one can make—even whole strings of errors, following false leads and/or not following leads carefully enough—on the way to satisfactory solutions. To complicate matters further, parts of many scientific puzzles may be missing or intermeshed with others and, even for those available, scientists have to sort out which parts form a coherent pattern and which are irrelevant. In addition, whereas pieces of a jigsaw puzzle do not change and normally fit together in only one way, the events that scientists seek to explain can and often do change—and may be explained in several ways.

In conducting their research, scientists define the phenomena they study in ways that make possible the selection, objective observation, and quantification of these phenomena; study changing relationships between events; and express the lawfulness of such changes mathematically (whenever possible). Mathematics, including statistics, helps one think about and investigate the relation of evidence and hypotheses. In fact, statistical inference is the connection between data and theory.

Scientists utilize control groups for comparison; look for all relevant data, including those that refute as well as those that confirm their hypotheses; and make their observations in such a manner as to allow them to be confirmed by more than one observer. Conclusions, always stated probabilistically, are continually modified as new data become available, thereby leading to possible new insights into issues under study.

Fallacious thinking (misleading assumptions and arguments) may often occur in asking questions, making observations, and formulating answers and arguments in support of those answers. Such thinking is common in everyday life, but it can also occur in science. Indeed, the open nature of scientific research provides continuing opportunity for such thinking to be challenged. *Further, not all questions can be formulated or answered scientifically.* Such is the case when questions are phrased illogically or when the data needed to answer them cannot be obtained or scientifically measured. Similarly, one must be aware that answers to questions can be wrong if they are logically indefensible or if they are based on inadequate data.

Common fallacies include the belief that if there is a name, there must be some real thing corresponding to that name (for example, the "faculties" and "propensities"—such as benevolence, cunning, and vanity—invented by the phrenologists and ascribed to specific locations in the head); the related tendency to assume that a description is identical to the phenomenon described ("the map is not the territory"); and the "gambler's fallacy"—that is, the belief that in a series of independent trials with fixed probabilities, the outcome in any given trial will be influenced by the outcomes of the preceding trials.

Other common fallacies are mistaking correlation for cause (the fact that two variables are systematically related does not by itself establish cause; my dog barks each morning just before sunrise, but his bark does not cause the sun to rise); the related confusion of effect and cause (in fact, the light changes prior to sunrise may cause my dog to bark); and failing to appreciate that an answer arrived at in one situation may not be generalizable to similar but not identical situations.

Additionally, students should appreciate that scientific questions and the ways they are asked by individual scientists may differ, depending on the schools of interpretation to which the scientists belong. The phenomena that scientists select for observation, the kinds of questions they ask about them, and the differential weights they assign to evidence may be affected (even if unwittingly) by their theoretical orientation and differing values (including any economic, political, social, cultural, and/or religious biases), as well as by their selective preoccupation with events in their own time and situation. For example, the study of allegedly inherited ethnic, sexual, and racial differences in the United States (as well as elsewhere) was undertaken with the ending of slavery, the increase of immigration, and escalating demands of blacks, immigrants, and women for legal, educational, and occupational equality within the established social order. Just after World War II, many psychologists and sociologists became preoccupied with problems of mass obedience to authority—for example, studies of the "authoritarian personality," an interest stimulated by events in Nazi-occupied Europe.

Science differs from other approaches as a way of establishing beliefs. It limits itself to answering empirical questions; it is inherently provisional, open-ended, and self-correcting. As a consequence, our understanding of the physical and human worlds has changed and continues to change over time. Moreover, the points of view upon which we base our science do change, and students should be aware of the nature of and bases for such change. In nonauthoritarian societies, it is generally recognized that scientific knowledge and the scientific approach to understanding need not be incompatible with aesthetic, moral, or ethical values, or with religious beliefs. On the other hand, revelations and interpretations of doctrinaire texts and decrees are influential in defining truth and providing meaning and solace for large portions of the world's population. Especially in more authoritarian settings, advocates of such beliefs attempt to constrain the thoughts and behavior of others through social or governmental control; and they consider scientific openness—particularly in matters of a social, political, or ethical nature—to be dangerous.

SOME CHALLENGES IN SOCIAL AND BEHAVIORAL SCIENTIFIC RESEARCH

What has been said so far holds for all areas of scientific inquiry. There are, however, some important problems that present special challenges to those who do research on social and behavioral phenomena.

First, *living things, and the systems they compose, progress through series of stages and phases, each of which results in changes in the kinds of response made to a given environment.* In addition, the characteristics of many of the phenomena of living beings, and particularly of human societies, typically are a function of their individual histories and of the larger circumstances in which they may happen to be observed (for example, the properties of the social phenomenon of "revolution" as studied in one phase, time, and place differ from those of "revolution" as studied in a different period and/or national heritage).

Second, *simply the reporting of social and behavioral phenomena by social scientists may influence the ways in which people behave. Sometimes the effect is to move people in the direction described or predicted by the social scientists, sometimes not.* An announcement of some new fact or process in the physical world (for example, the properties of a star) does not change that fact or process; however, an announcement of social science findings can lead to changes in the phenomenon being reported (for example, reports of the results of public opinion polling or test results can influence subsequent voting behavior or test-taking behavior).

Third, *when social scientists are present to observe the behavior of individuals or groups, their very presence may affect the behavior that is being observed* (for example, Margaret Mead's studies of native behavior in Papua permanently changed that culture; and segregation of groups of factory workers to study the effects of illumination on performance had a salutary effect independent of the level of illumination). Although the process of measurement can affect the phenomena that physical scientists seek to observe, the magnitude of the effects is generally quite small compared to what happens in the social sciences, where the magnitude may sometimes be large enough to cast doubt on the validity of the observations.

Fourth, *measurement problems in the social sciences are almost always complex.* We. speak of persons as being more or less intelligent, more or less afraid, more or less hungry, etc. Terms such as "more" or "less" imply that such attributes are measurable, even though there can be considerable difficulties in devising ways to measure them.

When social scientists look for factors that affect human behavior in the biology of the individual and the physical features of the environment in which the behavior occurs, they use the same units of measure as are used by physical scientists. (For example, in studies of the effect of noise or temperature upon the alertness of a human observer, noise is measured in decibels and temperature in degrees Celsius; further, such variables as alertness can also be measured by some quantitative index of performance, such as error rate; the same is true of economic indicators.)

However, when social scientists wish to measure the effect of social influence on psychological processes (for example, the influences of persuasion upon the political beliefs of a voter), a different kind of measurement problem arises. To establish that an argument presented by a person of high status has more influence than one presented by a person of low status, proper units need to be devised to measure status. We know in physics that 100 grams weighs twice as much as 50 grams, and that 100 grams is the same weight as the combined weight of two things that weigh 50 grams each. But is the status of the president twice that of a senator? Is it equal to the combined status of two senators? It may be fairly easy to decide which of two people has the higher status, but quite difficult to assign actual units to their status in the same way that we assign units to weight, height, or loudness.

In addition to the lack of common units or scales for measuring socially significant variables within a given culture, the situation is further confounded by the fact that many of the variables (such as status) are created by and vary with the social group in which they are found. Given the same atmospheric conditions, a burden of 20 kilograms requires the same muscular effort to lift in one culture as in another, but the social status accorded to a hermit living in poverty in one culture may be very different from that accorded in another.

Measurement of behavior is complicated still further by the fact that the ongoing activity of living organisms is seldom neatly divided into obviously separate responses, each with its own boundary. Defining where one response ends and the next one begins can be difficult (for example, in such activities as a bird building a nest, an individual expressing affection, a business corporation failing, or a political revolution beginning or ending) and is also subject to differences in theoretical interpretation. Sensory psychology and economics have more developed measurement schemes than other areas in the social sciences; sensory stimuli can be manipulated and tracked readily and precisely by the human observer, and many economic variables (for example, rates of change in gross national product [GNP]) can be stated in numerical terms.

Even when quantification is possible, however, some issues remain. For example, some methods of measurement (such as of intelligence) are based upon a theoretical assumption that the variable in question is normally distributed in the population at large, even though the assumption lacks empirical verification; and assignment of weights to components of compound measures (such as IQ and GNP) can be arbitrary and can selectively distort the meaning of the composite.

METHODS OF SCIENTIFIC INVESTIGATION

Categorization

Categorization—which is basic to language and thought processes and vital to science—involves the classification of objects and events into groups, on the basis of similarities or differences in one common attribute or more (any dimension on which an object or event can differ). Categorization permits us to systematically reduce large amounts of raw data to manageable proportions; go beyond information given (perceived) and infer common features among disparate objects, events, or ideas; and contrast and compare these objects. Categorization can occur in a variety of ways and at different levels of generality (for example, some categories are hierarchically organized, class-inclusive taxonomies—such as animal/mammal/dog/terrier; others are cross-classified—for example, father/son/uncle/Presbyterian/engineer). Categorization must be done carefully, because considerable information about each particular item is necessarily lost through grouping.

Categories in common usage are influenced by the cultural groups to which the categorizers themselves belong (religion, social status, nationality, etc.), and they acquire meanings from the situations in which they are frequently used and the particular purposes that they serve; thus, they differ, more or less, from person to person and society to society. Some categories used in virtually every human culture (categories such as botanical species and colors), are based on relatively stable, physical properties. Other categories, although seemingly universal and "natural" (and treated accordingly), are more social or culture-bound (for example, wealth, beauty, and ownership), are affected by value systems and language usage, and are subject to change over time. *Scientists endeavor to develop standard categories that have equivalent meanings to other scientists, regardless of language and culture; and, even when the categories themselves are not value-free, scientists aspire to recognize this fact and to treat them as neutrally as possible.*

Categories are developed for convenience or for other particular purposes and are often improved or replaced with additional knowledge or with change in objective. The development of categories that have practical implications for social policy is quite common in the social sciences (for example, such categories as poverty, homelessness, unemployment, and mental illness).

It is often difficult to define categories in ways that clearly distinguish the entities that belong in a particular category from entities that do not. Sometimes, such groupings have to be somewhat arbitrary (for example, the choice of a particular income level to distinguish categories above and below "the poverty line," or the distinguishing of the "mentally ill" from the "not mentally ill" by the arbitrary—and potentially misleading—use of the criterion of those seeking or being referred for psychotherapy versus those who are not).

Data

Data are descriptions of observed events. They provide the source of scientific theories and the means of testing them. Theories guide the way data are collected (that is, what variables are to be measured and how and what variables are to be controlled). Data analysis is used to compare data with theory: The results of data analysis indicate ways in which theory might be modified to better account for the data. Various methods are used to obtain data. Data may be obtained through controlled experimentation, in which manipulated and nonmanipulated variables are compared under rigorously controlled conditions. When the phenomena that we wish to study cannot be reproduced adequately in the laboratory (such as economic trends or revolutions) or when ethical considerations preclude controlled experimentation (as of stress reactions to disaster), data can be simulated by the use of models (including computer models) or through field studies (observations made as systematically as possible in the settings in which the events occur). A number of physical sciences (for example, astronomy, geology, and meteorology), as well as many social and behavioral sciences, must rely on the study of variations in "real" settings to infer relationships among phenomena that cannot be manipulated.

Research investigations may be cross-sectional or longitudinal. Cross-sectional studies obtain data on many subjects at one point in time, or over a short period; they are common in experimental manipulations and in surveys. Longitudinal studies accumulate data on a stable sample of subjects over an extended period of time; this technique is particularly useful for the study of developmental and dynamic phenomena.

Data may be obtained either from concurrent observation or from records and traces of events that have happened (such as artifacts and written records left behind by past cultures, and the settings in which they are found). Such data may be derived from official statistical records, the reports of intensive small-sample field observations, field studies and surveys (for example, ethnographic and participants' observations), unique cases (for example, memoirs, clinical histories, and archeological finds), or broad historical studies.

Data-collection techniques differ in their degree of intrusiveness into the event being observed (and in the possible consequent contamination of results). Human beings often behave differently when they know or believe they are being observed, compared to when they are not observed. This fact challenges the investigator's ingenuity to devise a means of neutralizing this problem so as not to bias the results. Observers themselves may also contribute to potential bias (systematic error) in the process of collecting data. Methods used to minimize such bias include the replication of observations before generalizations are made on the basis of them, and the use of panels of trained observers. It is also important that different observers use language in the same way to limit and describe the same phenomena.

Sampling

Even the simplest of behavioral and social phenomena result from a complex of ongoing determining processes. Individuals and groups vary, one from another, as a result of their particular histories. Nevertheless, it is usually unnecessary to study every case. Representative samples of subjects and conditions of observation can be employed, provided that care is taken to establish that they are typical of the population in question. Random sampling, with appropriate stratification (grouping by subcategory), is one way to minimize bias in selection. *Although it is not always possible to avoid some form of sampling bias, statistical techniques can be used to evaluate the bias.* The larger the amount of variability within the samples under investigation, the larger the sample will have to be to obtain significant differences between groups.

Measurement

Measurement (for example, counting, ranking, and rating) is essential to the scientific method. Entities exhibit more or less of particular attributes (such as height, weight, I.Q., rage, kinship loyalty, or debt ratio). Scientists devise ways in which these variations can be measured and represented numerically so that they can be subjected to mathematical or statistical analysis.

Some attributes can be observed and measured directly in physical units (such as amount of savings, number of votes, reaction time, or conditioned responses). However, other attributes can be inferred only from observable indices for which measurements can be devised, either from reports of subjects (for example, of images, feelings, attitudes, or expectations) or from samples of specific behavior (for example, "anger" inferred from amount of scolding, violent cursing, physical abuse, or changes in blood chemistry; "hunger" inferred from the rate at which a given amount of food is eaten, the amount of food eaten in a given time interval, or the amount of effort or punishment a subject will undertake or endure to obtain food; and "intelligence" inferred from vocabulary level, verbal comprehension, immediate recall of a set of presented stimuli, speed and accuracy of copying a complicated design, etc.).

Components may represent different aspects of the composite entity being measured. It is important to determine the extent to which component indices are equivalent so that quantities of one can be related to quantities of another. *To be useful, measurement must be reliable* (that is, yield the same value consistently and/or on repeated occasions) *and valid* (namely, measure that which it purports to measure).

Scientific Prediction

Scientific prediction varies in degree of accuracy. A scientist may fail to obtain a predicted outcome (prediction error) because there has been a failure to identify relevant variables in the first place; inaccuracy in measurement; or confounding of the contributions of converging variables. Progress in science (improvement of prediction) is achieved through successive refinements in all these areas. Patterns of overt behavior typically arise from differing combinations of variables, some of which are difficult to measure or even to detect. Thus, predictions must take into account varying degrees of uncertainty and must be made in actuarial terms.

Statistical Concepts

Statistical concepts are used to characterize various aspects of measured attributes within and between groups or categories. The difference between the lowest and highest measure is the range, which is one measure of variance; the ranked measures obtained by members of a group make up the distribution within that range. Differences on a particular attribute, whether within or between groups, may be expressed in terms of the range and the distribution of scores within that range, or in relation to a measure of central tendency or average score. The latter measure may be the arithmetic average (mean), the central or midmost measure (median), or the single score appearing most frequently (mode) in each group.

If the distribution of measures within the total range is "normal" (symmetrical about the central tendency), the mean, median, and mode should be approximately the same. On the other hand, if the distribution of measures is nonsymmetrical (skewed), the three "average" measures will be different. Such may be the case if the earnings of teenagers are measured. Here, a few successful entrepreneurial teenagers may have relatively high earnings (inflating mean income), many may have earnings in the middle of the range (determining median income), and more may have no earnings at all (thus setting the modal income at zero).

Statistical analyses are generally used to estimate properties of a population on the basis of a sample or to determine the likelihood that two or more samples could have been drawn from the same population; to evaluate the potential for error in such estimates; and to assess the probabilities of a given set, or sets, of possible outcomes and the likelihood that results that are obtained are not due to chance (that is, they are statistically significant). Scientific conclusions from observations require that the significance of observed relationships be assessed with the use of statistical confidence levels.

Findings that are actuarially (probabilistically) true may be used to predict for groups with confidence, but can be applied in individual cases only with due caution. For example, one cannot predict which particular individuals, amongst all drivers, will have an automobile accident; however, since it is actuarially true that a larger percentage of male drivers under the age of 26 are involved in automobile accidents than either female drivers of any age or male drivers over 26, insurance companies use the actuarial findings to charge all male drivers under 26 a higher premium than other individuals. Similarly, although it is not possible to identify in advance the particular individuals who will actually develop emphysema or lung cancer, doctors will be more likely to order chest x rays for patients who smoke than for those who do not, in that cigarette smokers actuarially are more likely than nonsmokers to develop those diseases.

Findings that are not statistically significant are not ordinarily regarded as valid—although that does not prove them invalid. On the other hand, since with very large samples the statistical significance of trivial effects is increased, some findings can attain statistical significance without having any substantive significance, "meaning," or utility.

TEACHING NOTES

It is difficult if not impossible to teach the principles of science without examples chosen both to illustrate the issues being presented and to be of interest to the majority of students. Many study modules can be developed around socially significant major themes. This is true in empirical social and behavioral science research at all levels, from biopsychology to cultural anthropology, political science, economics, and history. Each module can focus on question framing, research design, experimentation, and/or systematic observation, and interpretation of results and their implications, enhanced by discussion and debate about controversial issues (theoretical, methodological, and ethical).

Interesting lesson plans can be developed around the differences between pseudoscience and the social and behavioral sciences, for instance, by using examples of pseudoscience critiqued by the rigorous standards of scientific research.[4]

Following are four examples of socially significant study modules that can be developed to illustrate how scientific studies in various areas of the social and behavioral sciences are planned, conducted, and interpreted.

Example No. 1. The study of investigations of biopsychological processes can serve to illustrate the links between the brain and neuroendocrine systems on the one hand and between motivation and behavior dynamics on the other.[5] Studies of perceptual phenomena—such as constancy, geometric illusions, and perception of motion—are intrinsically interesting and lend themselves to laboratory exercises, demonstrations, and discussion about interpretations of the environment.[6]

Example No. 2. The following set of experiments and observations illustrates the empirical bases for the general conclusion that infants require attachment (including nurture, affection, and protection) and experience with others to thrive, physically and psychologically, and to develop into normally functioning members of social groupings. They also illustrate the bases for the significance of cultural and economic constraints on maternal attitudes and child survival.

Source materials on animal research with respect to controlled laboratory experimentation include the following:

- Harlow, H. F. 1959. "Love in Infant Monkeys." *Scientific American* offprint no. 429. New York: W. H. Freeman.

- Harlow, H. F., and M. K. Harlow. "Social Deprivation in Monkeys." *Scientific American* offprint no. 473. New York: W. H. Freeman.

Source materials on animal research with respect to longitudinal field observations include the following:

- Goodall, J. 1986. *Patterns of Behavior.* Cambridge, Mass.: Harvard University Press.

Source materials on human research with respect to longitudinal field observations include the following:

- Bowlby, J. 1973. *Attachment and Loss.* New York: Basic Books.

---

[4] See, for example, Wallis R., ed. 1979. *On the Margins of Science: The Social Construction of Rejected Knowledge, Sociological Review* monograph no. 27. See also Gardner, M. 1986. *Fads & Fallacies in the Name of Science.* New York: New American Library.

[5] See, for example, Pfaff, D. W. 1982. *The Physiological Mechanisms of Motivation.* New York: Springer-Verlag.

[6] See, for example, Rock, I. 1984. *Perception.* New York: W. H. Freeman.

- Macfarlane, J. W., L. Allen, and M. P. Honzik. 1954. *A Developmental Study of the Behavioral Problems of Children Between Twenty-one Months and Fourteen Years.* Berkeley: University of California Press.

- Werner, E. E., and R. S. Smith. 1982. *Vulnerable but Invincible.* New York: McGraw-Hill.

- Scheper-Hughes, N. 1984. "Infant Mortality and Infant Care: Cultural and Economic Constraints on Nurturing in Northeast Brazil." *Social Science and Medicine* 19:535–46.

- Scheper-Hughes, N. 1985. "Culture, Scarcity and Maternal Thinking: Maternal Detachment and Infant Survival in a Brazilian Shantytown." *Ethos* 13:291–317 (Stirling Award Essay, 1985).

- Scheper-Hughes, N. 1987. "The Cultural Politics of Child Survival" (book introduction). Pp. 1–31 in *Child Survival: Anthropological Perspectives on the Treatment and Maltreatment of Children*, N. Scheper-Hughes, ed. Dordrecht, the Netherlands: D. Reidel Publishing.

Example No. 3. Other study projects might focus on solutions to problems of defining and measuring psychological, sociological, and cultural attributes (for example, intelligence, vocational aptitudes, values, political opinions, social and cultural identities, and bases of stereotyping and ethnocentrism). Attention can be centered on the assumptions underlying common measures of these attributes, how such measures interrelate with each other, how they correlate with other variables, and the circumstances under which they were developed.[7]

Example No. 4. A recent report in *Science* would serve very nicely to illustrate the social science approach to problems—in this case, one bearing on social policy. The problem is that of estimating the composition and size of the population of the urban homeless people. The authors specified how they defined "urban homeless"; how they applied modern sampling methods to the study of the homeless to estimate the size of the homeless population; how they identified and measured the characteristics (mental and physical health, income, etc.) of the sample of the homeless they obtained; and, finally, how these characteristics compare with those of the general adult population.[8]

Similar study modules can and should be developed to illustrate additional problems and the ways in which scientists investigate them in other areas of the social and behavioral sciences, such as political science, economics, geography, and linguistics.

---

[7] See, for example, Anastasi, A. 1982. *Psychological Testing.* 5th ed. New York: Macmillan. See also Brown, R. 1986. *Social Psychology.* New York: Free Press.

[8] Rossi, P. H. et al. 1987. "The Urban Homeless: Estimating Composition and Size." *Science* 235:1336–41.

APPENDIX B

SOCIAL AND BEHAVIORAL SCIENCES PANEL CONSULTANTS

Herbert P. Baker   Social Studies Teacher, Belmont High School (Belmont, Massachusetts)

Roger Brown   Chaired Professor of Psychology, Harvard University

Paul W. Carey   Head of Social Studies Department, Belmont High School (Belmont, Massachusetts)

Lily Gardner Feldman   Associate Professor of Political Science, Tufts University

Richard Herrnstein   Edgar Pierce Professor of Psychology, Harvard University

Jacob Irgang   Social Studies Teacher, Stuyvesant High School (New York City)

Brendan A. Maher   Chaired Professor of Psychology, Harvard University

Joseph S. Nye, Jr.   Professor of International Security, John F. Kennedy School of Government, Harvard University

Orlando Patterson   Professor of Sociology, Harvard University

David Riesman   Professor Emeritus of Sociology, Harvard University

Edward E. Smith   Professor of Psychology, University of Michigan

Robert M. Solow   Institute Professor of Economics, Massachusetts Institute of Technology

Janet Spence   Professor of Psychology, University of Texas at Austin

James Stellar   Professor of Psychology, Northeastern University

Sidney Verba   Professor of Political Science, Harvard University

Ezra F. Vogel   Chaired Professor of Sociology, Harvard University

Myron Weiner   Professor of Political Science, Massachusetts Institute of Technology

NOTICE

This is one of five panel reports that have been prepared as part of the first phase of Project 2061, a long-term, multiphase undertaking of the American Association for the Advancement of Science designed to help reform science, mathematics, and technology education in the United States.

The five panel reports are:

• *Biological and Health Sciences: Report of the Project 2061 Phase I Biological and Health Sciences Panel*, by Mary Clark

• *Mathematics: Report of the Project 2061 Phase I Mathematics Panel*, by David Blackwell and Leon Henkin

• *Physical and Information Sciences and Engineering: Report of the Project 2061 Phase I Physical and Information Sciences and Engineering Panel*, by George Bugliarello

• *Social and Behavioral Sciences: Report of the Project 2061 Phase I Social and Behavioral Sciences Panel*, by Mortimer H. Appley and Winifred B. Maher

• *Technology: Report of the Project 2061 Phase I Technology Panel*, by James R. Johnson

In addition, there is an overview report, entitled *Science for All Americans*, which has been prepared by the AAAS Project 2061 staff in consultation with the National Council on Science and Technology Education.

For information on ordering all six reports, please contact Project 2061, the American Association for the Advancement of Science, 1333 H Street NW, Washington, D.C. 20005.